CULTURAL WEAP(

# Cultural Weapons

## Scotland and Survival in a New Europe

Christopher Harvie

**Polygon**
EDINBURGH

©   Christopher Harvie 1992
First Published by Polygon
22 George Square
Edinburgh EH8 9LF

Typeset by Cairns Craig Editorial, Edinburgh
Printed and bound in Great Britain
by Redwood Press Ltd, Melksham, Wiltshire

British Library Cataloguing in Publication Data
Harvie, Christopher
  Cultural Weapons, Scotland and Survival in a New Europe
  I. Title
  337.142

  ISBN   0 7486 6122 0

The Publisher acknowledges subsidy
from the Scottish Arts Council towards
the publication of this volume.

# Contents

An Economic Heresy
What Sort of a Life?
The Condition of England
Detmold, and a Late Score

To Alison and her friends at Grundschule im Aischbach, Tübingen, and Hanover School, Islington, London, for it will be their Europe, and in memory of Martin Spencer.

# Acknowledgements

I can no longer thank Martin Spencer, to whom my greatest debt is due, for having commissioned this book and argued the author out of some of his more outlandish intentions. He is lost to this forest, but not before he had stuck in many promising trees. My thanks to Marion Sinclair and her staff at Polygon for their patience in dealing with a remote and dilatory author.

Some sections of this book had their origins in articles written for the press, and I'm grateful to the editors of *The New Statesman*, *Planet*, *The Scotsman*, *Scotland on Sunday*, *The Times Higher Education Supplement*, and *The Western Mail*, for permission to reprint these. I must also express personal thanks for the co-operation I've had over the years from John Lloyd and Stuart Weir, Ned Thomas and John Barnie, Bob Campbell, Peter Jones and Jim Seaton, Brian Groom, Peter Aspden and Huw Richards, and Robin Reeves. At the BBC Ken Cargill, John Milne, Douglas MacLeod, and Colin Bell played a similar function, and elements of Part I stem from a diary which I kept during the making of the documentary *Grasping the Thistle* for the series *Scotland 2000*.

'Homage to Aschersonia' and parts of 'Sarter's Folly' first appeared in the *Times Higher Education Supplement*, 'The Future Thatcher Lost', 'On the Balance' and 'Talking of Auto-da-fees . . . ' in *Scotland on Sunday*; 'Lava on the Grass' in the *New Statesman*, 'Departures' in the *Western Mail* and the *Scotsman*, which also published parts of 'From Blut und Boden to Country and Western'. My thanks to all the editors for permission to reprint.

Some of the themes of *Cultural Weapons* are dealt with in greater detail in a Fabian Tract, *Against Metropolis*, of 1982 and in two contributions to *Political Quarterly* symposia 'Thoughts on the Union between Law and Opinion, or Dicey's Last Stand' in Colin Crouch and David Marquand (eds), *The New Centralism*, and 'English Regionalism: the Dog that Never Barked' in Bernard Crick (ed.), *National Identities*, both Blackwell, 1989 and 1991 respectively.

Another element has been papers delivered to conferences or

symposia, some of which have already been reproduced as 'proper' learned articles. In this context I must express my thanks to Professors Ludwig and Fietz at Tübingen, Alfred Braun of the Friedrich-Ebert-Stiftung, Dr Roland Sturm of Universtät Heidelberg, Dr Rainer Schulze of Ruhr-Universität Bochum, Dr Elmar Brandt of the Goethe-Institut, London, Neil Evans of Coleg Harlech, Professor Duncan Forrester of New College, Edinburgh, David Fletcher of *Transpennine*, and Hamish Morrison of the Scottish Council: Development and Industry.

In Tübingen my assistants, Carola Ehrlich and Paddy Bort, have contributed, in word-processing and translating, a compelling combination of the Swabian work-ethic and *joie de vivre*. I am also particularly grateful to my regional economics students, for bringing my more imaginative flights down to earth. To Tom Nairn, Neal Ascherson, John Osmond, Bernard Crick, Tom Gallagher, David Gow, Cairns Craig, Alex Salmond and Jim Sillars, David Marquand and Colin Crouch, thanks for arguments and stimulus – and apologies to Dafydd Elis Thomas, Kenneth Morgan, Ieuan, Maisie and Alun Gwynedd Jones, Miss Sophia Thomas and Phil Williams that Wales, where I've been made to feel so much at home, doesn't figure more. My wife Virginia and daughter Alison kept this *Scotus Viator* going, and have been marvellously tolerant of his disappearances to conferences and hurried journeys, and my sister Jane, Aunt Jessie and parents have provided my Scottish bases. Thanks to them all.

# Series Preface

Scotland's history is often presented as punctuated by disasters which overwhelm the nation, break its continuity and produce a fragmented culture. Many felt that 1979, and the failure of the Devolution Referendum, represented such a disaster: that the energetic culture of the 1960s and 1970s would wither into the silence of a political wasteland in which Scotland would be no more than a barely distinguishable province of the United Kingdom.

Instead, the 1980s proved to be one of the most productive and creative decades in Scotland this century – in literature, in thought, in history, creative and scholarly work went hand in hand to redraw the map of Scotland's past and realign the perspectives of its future. In place of the few standard conceptions of Scotland's identity, a new and vigorous debate was opened up about the nature of Scottish experience, about the real social and economic structures of the nation, and about the ways in which the Scottish situation related to that of other similar cultures throughout the world.

It is from our determination to maintain a continuous forum for such debate that *Determinations* takes its title. The series provides a context for sustained dialogue about culture and politics in Scotland, and about those international issues which directly affect Scottish experience.

Too often, in Scotland, a particular way of seeing our culture, of representing ourselves, has come to dominate our perceptions because it has gone unchallenged – worse, unexamined. The vitality of the culture should be measured by the intensity of debate which it generates rather than the security of ideas on which it rests. And should be measured by the extent to which creative, philosophical, theological, critical and political ideas confront each other.

If the determinations which shape our experience are to come from within rather than from without, they have to be explored and evaluated and acted upon. Each volume in this series seeks to be a contribution to that *self*-determination; and each volume, we trust, will require a response, contributing in turn to the on-going dynamic that is Scotland's culture.

CAIRNS CRAIG

The only communication between man and man
That says anything worth hearing
 – The hidden well-water; the finger of destiny –
Moves as that water, that angel, moved.
Truth is the rarest thing and life
The gentlest, most unobtrusive movement in the world.
I cannot speak to you of the poor people of all the world
But among the people in these nearest slums I know
This infinitesimal twinkling, this delicate play
Of tiny signs that not only say more
Than all speech, but all there is to say,
All there is to say and to know and to be.
There alone I seldom find anything else,
Each in himself or herself a dramatic whole,
An 'agon' whose validity is timeless.
Our duty is to free that water, to make these gestures,
To help humanity to shed all else,
All that stands between any life and the sun,
The quintessence of any life and the sun;
To still all sound save that talking to God;
To end all movements save movements like these.
India had that great opportunity centuries ago
And India lost it – and became a vast morass,
Where no water wins free; a monstrous jungle
Of useless movement; a babel
Of stupid voices, drowning the still small voice.
It is our turn now; the call is to the Celt.

Hugh MacDiarmid, 'A Glass of Pure Water'

# Introduction:
# With the Magic Rucksack

## I

After Bietigheim the sky, which in Stuttgart had been clear, suddenly darkened and blotted out an April summer. Snow pelted the blossom on the fruit trees, covered tennis-courts, dissolved on already-filled swimming pools. The country went sullen, power-cables and parked cars stood out. A factory chimney soared into the grey. Somehow, this seemed an appropriate atmosphere in which to give the book its final shape.

I first thought about this book in 1988, largely wrote it between 1989 and 1990. I wrote in a Europe which was in constant change: first gradual, then with a confident, democratic optimism, and finally at a precipitate, incalculable rate which could only provoke alarm. In April 1991 the snow was on the blossom; in the summer both held on, fear outweighed hope.

To say that this book will be difficult to classify is to ask for it. It is partly contemporary history: an attempt to make sense of recent events, partly a discussion of political strategy, but also an attempt to locate a particular *mentalité*. It is written by a commuter between centre and periphery in Europe; by a historian whose 'serious' work is aimed at only a few others, but who also sustains the above life by journalism; by a socialist horribly fascinated by the protean qualities of modern capitalism, but convinced of its decadence. It is prophecy and warning, which is always dodgy ground to stray on to.

I like to think that all of these factors may more than add up, and help produce what Patrick Geddes called 'synergy': the new and stimulating dialectic that Scotland, in her present situation, needs. The urgency of the journalist – the need to locate specific events on a short time-scale – *may* energise the more deliberate methods of the historian. Both may react with my economic analysis to suggest ways in which 'Scotland in Europe' – an attractive but so far still essentially a constitutional proposition – may take on deeper social, political and cultural dimensions.

1

'Synergy' and provocation don't sit easily with the laws and usages of the profession: generalising only after you have accumulated a mass of material. A J P Taylor, always a stimulating if dangerous role-model, a kindly and approachable man much missed, loved being a polemical journalist, but wrote that he had never actually suggested the subject of any one of his serious history books. They had always been the result of commissions. Taylor, however, wrote out of a great tradition of British diplomatic and political history; anyone dealing with modern Scotland has to take the initiative – however embarrassing that might be.

This was even more the case when it came to making sense of new European political movements. In 1980, despite Britain's adherence to the European Communities, the mind of the United Kingdom was insular as never before. To get involved oneself in German culture and politics, particularly at the important *Land* level, was to venture into an area neglected both by metropolitan journalists and by the *illuminati* of the Königswinter conferences. On the other hand, this simultaneous involvement with German politics and the cause of Scottish autonomy generated a dialogue which got steadily more important as the decade wore on.

What abilities could I bring to this? Historians, unlike theoretical physicists, don't burn themselves out by middle age. Provided our memories are up to it, a pretty effective filing system should accumulate a 'pile' of information bubbling away, not difficult to tap into. Further, I had a series of research projects behind me which had centred on the role of the intelligentsia as political interpreters – and a fascination with communications technology. This 'pile' was different from the one that powered Taylor. My *polis* was a lot smaller – states and communities in Scotland, London, Wales, South Germany. If one was hopeful, it was – now – more relevant, as it covered the making of a civil society which could utilise a mixed economy or a social market to solve horrendous world problems. If one wasn't hopeful, one landed back with Taylor's northern radical's view of nationalism as *sacro egoismo*, Germany's being the biggest and worst. Taylor denied that history had any pattern – 'Napoleon III studied history' – I can still hear that sharp Mancunian-Oxford voice – 'and learned from the mistakes of the past how to make new ones.' On the other hand he was emotionally drawn to great system-makers: Marx and Engels, Beaverbrook and the Empire. He campaigned against what he saw as the threat of world-suicide through nuclear weapons, yet he produced no historical arguments to back his stand. He abstained from the debate about whether history is scientific or imaginative, whether it's an experimental model or an epic poem. I believe it has to be both: it has to be a structure in which one tests hypotheses about social development – particularly at the present time, because if we get the tests wrong, we won't be able to retake them. We have seen what is claimed to be the bankruptcy of the Marxist model, brought down, at least in part, by impulses which were poetic, dramatic and religious. At the same time, 'triumphant' liberal capitalism is itself badly flawed as a system, sunk in a primitive acquisitive materialism, incapable either of envisaging the scale of the techno-economic changes which have engulfed it, or of bringing the frequently irrational human responses to these changes under control.

'It is our turn now; the call is to the Celt'. If I have MacDiarmid's poem 'A Glass of Pure Water' in mind, it is for two reasons. MacDiarmid, like Taylor, reminds me how epigonic my generation is, how much we depend, for our more important perceptions, on standing on the shoulders of such men. The title of this book reflects an advantage that the British nations still possess, through the continuity of cultural and social argument that they maintained, when that of Europe was shattered by the events of 1933-45. However besmirched by the last decade, this confidence in society – that, in Tom Johnston's words, 'what men do together, they *can* do' – still contrasts with a European order essentially kept together by law. Properly developed, it can release energies which Europe badly needs.

'A Glass of Pure Water' also captures a fundamental dilemma – and a chance for Scotland. The motives behind the drive for Scottish autonomy are inchoate – the loss of manufacturing and industrial control, the problems of social deprivation, the ambitions of a post-imperial political elite. Granted autonomy, they could still confuse and betray each other. Yet a community struggling through a particularly deformed industrial experience towards the responsibilities of statehood has learned important lessons, and ought to be able to teach. MacDiarmid's poem is Blakeian in its juxtaposition of the intimate and the immense, profoundly Christian in its sense of the universality of God's love; yet written by an atheist and materialist. It strengthens my belief that those collectively unnameable countries – the Celtic fringe, the British periphery – have, in their dialogue with England, developed possible answers to the problems of a rich and troubled continent, and of the impoverished millions who starve and struggle beyond its frontiers. If this is blatant ideology, so much the better – as long as it does what ideology is supposed to do, and provokes.

## II

The title of this introduction refers to my constant companion. For the last few years, as well as teaching German students about *Landeskunde Größbritanniens und Irlands* – or British and Irish cultural studies, I have reported on European affairs for various papers in Britain. In this the laptop computer has been a boon and a blessing, and has obviously altered the way in which one writes and presents and attempts to persuade. I am still trying to work out the full implications of being able to carry an office-full of books and articles about on a few discs, of being able, by cheap fax and phone, to make something happen, some opinion count, at the other end of Europe. On a personal level I have been able – though I may flatter myself – to affect Scottish affairs more than I would have been, had I lived in Scotland for the last decade. Two of the things I have struggled for: Scottish self-government and a rational transport policy, are far closer to realisation than they looked in 1979 . . .

A voice: You're havering. Who the hell's ever heard of you?
CTH: Well, I made *Grasping the Thistle* for the BBC in 1986, and I think that had some effect in getting the devolution business on the go.
Punter (for it is he): You put everyone to sleep. Donald Dewar said in 1988 'Professor Who?'
CTH: That was when I campaigned for Jim Sillars in Govan. Look what happened there. Anyway, a lot of people in Scotland would ask 'Donald who?'
Punter: I'll grant you that. But no-one's going to storm out on to the streets demonstrating about a Scottish Assembly. Where do they put it in the polls when they list their priorities? About seventh? In February 1988 people like me were watching *Tutti-Frutti*, not you.
CTH: But *Tutti-Frutti* makes my point. This was good social-critical stuff. It was Scotland intellectually up and running. If you mention the words *Tutti-Frutti* on the continent people think it means a quiz show with a half-naked girl being asked where the Eiffel Tower is.
Punter: But that's what people want. Remember H L Mencken: 'Nobody ever lost money by underestimating the taste of the

great American public.' And all this guff about the 'mission' of the Scots. Look at Rupert Murdoch, Andrew Neil, Kelvin MacKenzie. People talk about rubbish. We produce it.

CTH: Now *you're* coming the intellectual. Yes, I am worried about gutter newspapers and gutter TV reducing people to a zombie level, because we are creating appalling social, economic and ecological problems for ourselves and at the same time dismantling the equipment that people need to master them.

Punter: Lord Reith rides again!

CTH: Better Reith than Murdoch. We now have Murdoch in Germany. He's set up a paper called *Super* in East Berlin. If you thought *Bild-Zeitung* was bad, this makes *Bild* look like the *Church Times*: 'Hop off Wessi Wankers' is roughly its tone.

But this is a struggle within *our* culture: Jekyll and Hyde, the Justified Sinner . . .

Punter: So how does this book help, beyond introducing us to the prejudices of a train-travelling dominie?

CTH: It suggests that if Scotland is going to survive in Europe it shouldn't just copy institutions in, say, Germany. It should find out the points where, through drawing on its strengths, and combating its weaknesses, it can fit itself into the most critical areas of change in Europe, and trade from this position. So I'm going to start with general European change, then look at Germany, and see where Scotland could fit in.

Punter: All the time hectoring us?

CTH: You heard what I said. If you don't like it, you can always argue back.

# 1 'In the Interstices of History'

'Wales, as a nation, lives in the interstices of other people's history.'

(Gwyn A Williams)

## Mourning Becomes Euphoria

### I

Commentaries on the state of Europe in the 1970s were almost unrelievedly gloomy. In 1979 Walter Laqueur, the doyen of European contemporary history, wrote that 'the recent history of Europe could be written in the categories of clinical psychology; if individuals suffer from clinical disorders, so too do groups of people'. A decade later, this gave way to a sort of 'market euphoria'. The *Angst*-creators of the 1970s – unemployment, inflation, drugs, terrorism – hadn't gone away. In fact they had now teamed up with Aids, global warming, the Chernobyl effect, the depletion of the ozone layer, Moslem fundamentalism and a revival of national egoism. But people felt better.

In 1987 one of my academic contemporaries, the historian Paul Kennedy, in *The Rise and Fall of Great Powers*, put the black spot on his adoptive homeland, the United States, and made a lot of money therefrom. But it was the old enemy, Soviet Russia, which promptly dived into crisis. Two years later Kennedy's book was being pushed from the airport bookstall shelves by Francis Fukuyama's claim that market liberalism and democratic pluralism were the unqualified victors of the ideological battle of the century. 'History', in the dialectical sense of Hegel and Marx, was now at an end.

As East Europe went to real elections for the first time in fifty years or more, this faith in the market seemed to swell, at least in those states whose economics and political culture were closest

6

to the 'developed' west. This verged on the absurd when Western leaders famed for economic ineptitude and power-obsession came, like mad Pretenders in Mussorgsky operas, attended by choruses of desperate, credulous *Moujiks*, to bathe in the approval of liberated East Europeans. It became chillingly obvious that the symbols of what the East wanted – fast food, cars, television – was what more sensible elements in the West considered themselves as surfeited and endangered by.

'It was the best of times. It was the worst of times.' The Communist framework fell apart, but economic failure shadowed the West. Dickens' flourish in *A Tale of Two Cities* seemed apt. The United States and Great Britain, which together had saved the liberal world order in war, and created the paradigms of enterprise for the West, were unhealthy, as societies and economies. Britain, after ten years of Thatcherite 'radicalism', was in many respects less competitive than it had ever been, its society bitterly divided and disoriented; the United States, with only nine years of its own fuel supplies to go, was threatened with vast budget and trade deficits, crime, drugs and – as the Savings and Loan issue showed – financial malpractice on an incredible scale. The real initiative rested with the defeated powers – Germany and Japan – still excluded from the UN security Council and by definition precluded from 'teaching the lessons' which usually followed material success.

## Comparative Children, or Boris and Steffi in the Dark Wood

A boy got on to the Bonn-Stuttgart train. He was about sixteen, large, blond and overweight, dressed in a violently-coloured pink, green and purple T-shirt, baggy jeans and floppy, elaborate trainers. A Walkman pumped decibels into his pink ears. He produced a bag of sweets and ate them, reading as he did so a Donald Duck comic. The sweets finished, he lit the first of several cigarettes. Outside, the vineyards and castles of the Rhine gorge slipped past, unseen. He removed one ear-piece and the rhythm section blasted out. A severe-looking old lady raised her eyes skywards.

*Die Zeit* magazine reminded me – along with its other *anständige Deutsche* readers, church-people, academics, party members, civil servants – with a German combination of high seriousness and good photography, of skeletal bodies and sad, wise-looking heads: dying children in refugee camps: 'Am I not a man and a brother?' Somewhere else in our society was this boy – acoustically quarantined from the world about him. Could he even articulate such a notion? Or only embody the passivity of the Western consumer?

Was that what the old lady was registering? Or was he just aesthetically repellent, American, *fremd* . . . ? Was she concerned that such overt mindlessness seemed to show, all too easily, a systematic limitation of human potential? At the evolution of a sort of consuming animal, devouring a cultural pap programmed to minimise any sort of response, let alone a political one?

What would she rather have had him be? A neat idealistic Storm-Trooper, his head filled with Nordic myth? One of Honecker's Free German Youth, ready to shop his parents to the Stasi? What was *her* background, anyway? Could one see, in her reaction, the thought that the boy was *not Boris*? Cast an eye at what's called the 'rainbow press' in any German newsagent, running from soft porn to *People's Friend* sentimentalism, and you find Boris and Steffi, the Hansel and Gretel of German tennis – form, friends, fears, families, money. At one level this is *Rentnerfutter* – 'pensioners' fodder'. For an elderly generation with very few grandchildren Boris and Steffi were the great surrogates. On another level they were the free-enterprise West's response to the shock that it got in the 1960s when the German Democratic Republic, worse-off in every respect, beat it hollow in sport.

Boris and Steffi spearheaded a 'sport-wave' designed to provide a 'moral equivalent' to German military prowess, and an alternative to slumping into a deck-chair at Rimini or a couch in front of the television. Cash was injected into moribund *Turnverein*, gymnastic associations dating from the early days of the nationalist movement; playing fields were levelled, tennis courts laid out and swimming-pools dug. By 1990 Germany exceeded Britain in sport-obsession. More people played. The Monday papers were choked with endless sport reports. The sensation of July 1990, which had parties going on to all hours and cars hooting the night away, was not German unity but winning the World Cup.

Mass-consumerism and sport-patriotism were the anodyne values which replaced old, dangerous loyalties. For long enough they had no blood on their hands. But the feeling grew that they were themselves drugs, to fill – very unsatisfactorily – a mental and spiritual vacuum:

> But men betimes are sober,
> And think by fits and starts,
> And when they think they fasten
> Their hands upon their hearts.

Consumerism implied a retreat from society; sport a highly-restricted form of collective activity. My neighbours in the parents' group in Tübingen, classic Michael Frayn-style 'herbivores', could make little progress with the 'settlers' who flocked into our bit of town – Silesians, Roumanian Saxons, Volga Germans from Kazakstan. 'They don't come out, even when we put things on for them. They stick in their flats with the television on all night long. Television, video, a car, that's what Western civilisation means to them.'

European history is murky and homicidal, often in proportion to the strength of its idealism. Somewhere, during the Middle East emergency in some militant Arab training camp, German extremists of the far left Rote Armee Fraktion and the racist, anti-semitic right must have encountered one another *on the same side*. But the problem about a privatised, compartmentalised affluence is that it encourages the politically-discontented to form sects equally withdrawn from society, crazily convinced of their own rectitude yet competent enough in taking revenge. Between 1989 and 1991, in a noticeably unviolent society, the RAF killed the bosses of the biggest German bank and the reconstruction authority for East Germany; 'disturbed individuals' nearly killed the SPD chancellor candidate and the interior minister.

Sport and consumerism might work as placebos, while there's money and security, but if these reassurances decrease and real menaces appear they become dangerous. The internationalist impulses of socialism are now in abeyance, but the style of the English skinhead – aggressive, nationalistic, sectarian – has an 'international' appeal to insecure East German youth. The football crowd, splintering into confrontations with police and minority groups, could look disturbingly like the crucible of a new street-fighting Nazism.


## II


The travelling boy raised another issue. If one regarded the events of 1989–90 in the optimistic light of Ralf Dahrendorf or Timothy Garton Ash, the revolutions were a 'European', home-grown achievement: really the first such since the nineteenth century. From the days of Woodrow Wilson on, the United States had had to intervene to rescue Europe from its excesses. Now 'American-ism' – the very words 'land of unlimited possibilities' – increasingly seemed to posit this unacceptable, obese, materialist image. The Soviet utopia was in ruins, but the periodic renewal of the Republic had not arrived on cue. Fifteen years separated Versailles from the New Deal; fifteen years separated Roosevelt's death and Kennedy's election. But in 1990 Kennedy had been dead for nearly thirty years. The West German crowds who had responded to him in 1962 had transferred their enthusiasm to the figure of Mikhail Gorbachev, then to Helmut Kohl. These were Europeans – even if the first was the official receiver of a bankrupt empire, and the second a provincial frog blowing himself into an ox.

*Police Academy 5* – a lame-brain rerun of the Keystone Kops – was playing in Tübingen for its eleventh week, but the 'single European home' – Gorbachov's baroque experiment – had to be believable. Or was the European ideal merely a transient enthusiasm generated, like Thatcherite economic recovery, by the public relations machine? Anyone observing events on both sides of the Iron Curtain from a German university would be struck by a huge, ironic dislocation between information and *real* social and technological change: the hope invested in 'Europe' or 'markets' or 'society' and the vagueness in defining them.

We seemed to have reached one of those points of comprehensive economic and social alteration that Fernand Braudel identified – the last having been in the eighteenth century. Political changes were hirpling along in the wake of this. At the same time consciousness was limited, even reluctant: the youth attached to the Walkman, isolated from society *by* the technology that was turning it upside-down; the 'old' Germany of small town tradesmen and restaurants offering local food and market traders going on as if for ever, and then suddenly giving up. I sensed that a debate about change, community and politics, which had been going on in Scotland since the 1960s, had somehow got ahead of the European game, just when 'Europe' was formally creating space for the smaller European nations and their intimate politics of community and ecology.

A *reprise* of the 'matter of Scotland' in the eighteenth and nineteenth centuries was timely, because recovering and re-interpreting the Scottish past seemed to coincide with the renewed relevance of the Scottish 'idea' in Europe. The obvious figure seemed to be Adam Smith, the bicentenary of whose death was celebrated in 1990, yet contemporary changes and challenges went far beyond the economic liberalism touted as a panacea in East Europe. The programme of the new radical movements in areas like Czechoslovakia conjured up, in fact, the *opposition* to Smith in eighteenth century Scotland, Adam Ferguson's concentration on the 'civil society' which economic liberalism was seen as subverting. The escape from dogmatic Marxism and the restating of the goal of liberal economic development reawakened the debate about whether 'progress' was to be preferred to social cohesion; whether the solidarity of the pre-industrial community could be replaced by the fragile relationships of the market and of social class.

Scotland had, in the eighteenth century, loosed the dynamic of market society. This had had ambiguous consequences for the country, something reflected in the popularity of Burns and Walter Scott, who judged 'enlightenment' and 'improvement' by the Scots historical experience, and expressed doubts about their social implications. Perhaps the rapid development since the 1960s of Scottish history has provided one reason why, when others believe unquestioningly in markets, the Scots have been notably sceptical. But this still made it necessary to establish a continuum – a language, an historical approach – which linked the Scottish past to the present situation.

## Homage to Aschersonia

The frontier is now some distance behind, on the other side of the pine-woods, storm-battered and gnawed by the acid rain. A hare squats in the moss and tangled grass of the autobahn, built in Hitler's days and severed by the barbed wire. The railway gets through, though, a fifties diesel bucketing along the tracks, trailing battered dirty-green carriages, their smoky interiors occupied by literary dissidents, soldiers, one-legged accordionists and Alsatian dogs, and alert journalists with battered steam typewriters. Someone has blasted the eagle off the pediment of the *Grenzbahnhof*: bullet-marks still pock the grubby stucco. An old-young guard with a drooping moustache leaves his drink under the faded awning and clambers up for passports. He knows German; somehow, the seventy words of command have survived. 'Nicht Engländer – Schotte!' produces some effect: 'Glasgow Celtic? Ja?' He lets us through. Welcome to Aschersonia.

It is not at all easy to envisage the country from the capital, save as a place beyond the ranks of workers' flats at the end of the tramlines, where things seem to be seen differently, by different people. Different people, that is, from the Members of the Diet, or the habitues of the Government quarter and the Bourse, the posh restaurants, the Academy and the Opera. But people would say that 'real' life goes on in the Slav or Italian street cafés of the university quarter, where various academics and *Regime-Kritiker* argue for hours on coffee and Bulgarian wine, observed from time to time by morose representatives of the Secret Police. Those heavily-built young men, baffled by the torrent of concept and comparison and yawning into their rolled-up copies of the *Sport Digest*, seem to be the only functioning connection between metropolitan Aschersonia's two worlds.

The constitution is a puzzle. Where does the Monarchy end and the People's Republic begin? The gilded carriages rattle down from the Palace, the Black Guard of the regime struts to its drums, commemorating some victory or other over the Enemy – that remote, shadowy force, miles beyond the central plain, sometimes linked up with the miners in the mountains, sometimes with the nationalists. The Boulevard press tells you little beyond the endless *Klatsch* of the Court: the elderly, dour monarch, the golden princesses, the critical, slightly unnerving figure of the crown prince. The university quarter bothers as little with this as it does with the endless bulletins of government success, though these seem to be borne out by the glittering blocks on the Ringstrasse, the crowds of *nouveaux riches* in the big restaurants, and the neat suburbs on the south-facing slopes. Look beyond this place, they say. Forget the Kitsch and the press-releases. The activity of the regime is desperation not dynamism. The economy is in the pits and the country is breaking up. But a lot of them are from the People's Republic, and they would say that anyway, wouldn't they?

\* \* \*

It was Istvan Szabo's film *Colonel Redl* that triggered this off. Redl was a Ruthenian Jew who became a senior intelligence officer in the Habsburg empire before World War I. A super-patriot, he found that, once he got to the centre of Austrian power and influence, the whole imperial structure seemed simply to fall apart. In Szabo's film Redl, completely disillusioned, blurts out secrets to a Russian agent and is then forced to commit suicide. As a 'marginal' man he has structured his personality round the service of the state. When the state proves hollow, he has nowhere else to go.

To proceed from Redl to Malcolm Rifkind, Secretary of State for Scotland, seemed logical. Rifkind, Lithuanian-Jewish in origin, young, intelligent, is another 'marginal' man, this time in the caste-world of Scottish Conservatism, proving his 'Britishness' by 150% loyalty to the Thatcherite programme and, like Redl, sent back to manage his remote and disloyal province. This he does with skill, but the disloyalty grows, and he eyes the instability of the capital with disquiet. Should Thatcherism come unstuck – or even if it doesn't – Scotland is where the British state will start to unravel. For good.

This is unlikely to have the effect on Rifkind that it had on Redl. Rifkind is not in the least a tragic figure. But the comparison is important in that it locates the 'radicalism' of Mrs Thatcher at a precise historical juncture, as something less 'British' than comparable to the various, increasingly desperate, attempts the Austrian elite made to keep the empire together in the years between 1848 and the outbreak of World War I. The intriguing thing is that the geography of this has been sketched by a man of rather similar background to Rifkind.

No-one has pinned down the peculiarities of the British state more deftly than Neal Ascherson, in his *Observer* pieces and in the longer addresses which, from time to time, he targets at Scottish audiences. But one senses a slight bafflement among his metropolitan readers at the dimensions of his 'Ukania', a place which seems as peculiar, if as tangible, as 'Greene-land'. Is this really where we are, among Polish partisans and Czech historians who have somehow got mixed up with London journalists and with Scots poets and politicians?

The problem about 'Ukania' is that it describes a pathological state, which the patient isn't, of course, going to analyse. It's Ascherson's own adaptation from the pre-World War I Viennese satirist Karl Kraus's 'Kakania' (K.u.K.: Kaiserlich und Königlich) which, used thus, sounded – and was meant to sound – like 'Shit-state'. Kraus was Jewish but a militant partisan of the German language against the continual assaults which its integrity had to suffer through Austrian politics, court intrigue and financial speculation. He saw the Habsburg struggle for survival as literally 'the last days of mankind'. To Kraus the ultimate peril was that politics should capture the language, and mould it in such a way that objectivity was impossible. Moreover, this danger was aggravated by the continual instability of the Empire: the elite's application of one drastic remedy after another – selling state property, abolishing local systems of administration, granting autonomy to the Hungarians, intriguing with the South Slavs – without, it hoped, damaging its own control.

Like Kraus, and like another old-Etonian outsider, George Orwell, Ascherson's commitment to the integrity of language is total. But – part Scots, part Berlin Jew – he is too much on the periphery to share Orwell's identification with that 'British people', whom he took to be a rock of common-sense humanity in the tormented sea of inter-war European politics. It is, perhaps, less easy to believe this after 'Falklands fever' and the rise of the English tabloid press. 'Britain' has faded, and Ukania, a slicker, less thuggish version of Orwell's 'Airstrip One', has taken over.

But not for long. The geography of politics is changing. Ukania is slowly modulating into Europe – some parts of it more satisfactorily than others – and a new language is necessary to understand the *mentalités* of new fellow-citizens. The seventy words of command – English-style – are no longer adequate, and without this linguistic leap (difficult for a country so deficient in foreign language acquisition), English itself stands in danger of succumbing to an Americanised Newspeak. We encounter the Aschersonian frontier again around here, where free thinking and plain speaking are necessary to make a new, 'stretched' European *polis* tolerable. And yet, having adopted these values, the polis itself stretches further, grants citizenship to dissidents from East Europe, recognises bloody-minded little nationalities which embarrass the big nation-states and multinational companies. An inconvenient nation, Aschersonia, but one that has resonances. With the medieval Ghibellines and their notion of an elective Emperor and a conciliar Church, with the 'nations' of the Italian or Scots universities, or with the socialist community of the Second International (the centenary of which seems – all too inevitably – to have eluded Comrades Kinnock and Hattersley).

But back to the capital. Observe the lovingly-restored private train chugging off to show tourists the great houses of the provinces and the fascinating industrial theme parks, the theatres crammed with Andrew Lloyd-Webber productions; the auction houses getting incredible prices for the salon paintings of Victorian Academicians. The long view from the university quarter may be exhilarating, vertiginous: stretching and stressing the language, particularly when deployed by mutinous provincials. (Witness Gwyn Williams on the 'psychiatric' vocabulary of Tom Nairn, frequently to be encountered among the Ascherson partisans, ramming explosive shells of language into his Carlyle Mark II howitzer). But when, from time to time, these whistle over the boulevards, in the direction of the Palace, they only thud against the protective wadding of *Kitsch* and *Klatsch*.

For how long? Aschersonia's capital in exile is, of course, Vienna. Bourgeois and German, it fed itself on Sachertorte, Operetta and the pictures of Hans Makart, erected phoney palaces on the Ringstraße, trusted populist 'radical' politicians, with their convenient repertoire of 'enemies within'. More than a few Viennese – Freud, Herzl, Wittgenstein, Schoenberg – looked beyond, saw visions, and proposed grand, all-enveloping solutions. But common to both chancers and visionaries was a failure to anchor themselves in a tolerable, resilient civil society. On being informed that such and such an officer – Redl, maybe – was 'a patriot', the old Emperor remarked 'Yes, but is he a patriot for me?' If you can't have loyalty where several ideas of civil society are in competition, then the idea of civil society itself will tend to atrophy. As, under Mrs Thatcher, it has atrophied in Britain.

The intriguing thing is that the bony hand of the Habsburg Empire has reached out to scribble on the Downing Street desk. When their train bore the last Emperor and his family over the frontier in November 1918, Friedrich Hayek was nineteen, Karl Popper sixteen, Ludwig von Mises thirty-seven. The 'Austrian School' broods over Thatcherism, economists and social philosophers from the old Austro-German elite whose approach to society and politics rejected a fractured historical experience which contaminated any general metaphysical explanations of state and society. By contrast, the hegemony of the market economy appeared as something almost transcendent: a depoliticised heaven of theory, the economic analogue to Kraus's purified German or Mahler's musical vision. Popper continues to laud the Ukanian political system, when almost every other articulate commentator wants proportional representation, while Hayek, secure in Social-Democrat-run Freiburg, regards Thatcher as his most promising pupil. It sometimes seems, when one regards the Ukanian capital from the provinces, that the Old Kakanians, those who can still remember the Vienna of drastic solutions and desperate expedients, are playing their last, deadly joke.

## *The Uses of Prophecy*

### I

Victorian statesmen studied the classics and insisted that once you understood the politics, history and rhetoric of the Greek city states and the Roman republic, you could cope with most political situations. Scots enlightenment philosophers, attuned to the *fact* of social and economic change, were more defensive: aware that forces had been unleashed which had completely altered the social balance, and which men could no longer properly control. Their silence when the industrial process got into its stride is ominous; a philosophical analogue to those parts of Scottish cities where classical squares and crescents suddenly give way to the anarchy of Victorian factories, churches and slums.

But did the Enlightenment fall silent? One voice insists it did not.

> Men are grown mechanical in head and in heart, as well as in hand. They have lost faith in individual endeavour, and

in natural force, of any kind. Not for internal perfection, but for external combinations and arrangements, for institutions, constitutions – for Mechanism of one sort or another, do they hope and struggle.

Thomas Carlyle – a figure first encountered twenty-odd years ago, while I and others were putting together the 'Industrialisation and Culture' section of the Open University's first foundation course – has in the last few years thrust himself into my mind with increasing and insistent regularity. Partly because of parallel interests: Scotland, Britain and Germany; partly because of the imaginative power of his language, the compact significance of his metaphors for change and modernism, and partly also for qualities of irony, scepticism and moral urgency. Against these, our contemporary political rhetoric seemed sadly attenuated, in comparison with the work to be done.

When a historian tries to address the public on social change this language becomes important. This book grew out of work as a reporter, academic and conference-attender, over the last fifteen years, part of Carlyle's 'effective Church' – holding forth on new weapons to NATO generals and on the New Europe to Scottish industrialists, commenting on a landscape in upheaval from my 'balcony' in Germany, writing books and scripting TV programmes. Was this having some effect, or at the very least pushing history along the lines in which I thought it ought to be going? If so, how much was I working as a 'jobbing historian', or as a 'good communicator'?

I found myself assessing the relative value of these two roles when, in the autumn of 1989, I chaired a debate between Neal Ascherson and Hans-Magnus Enzensberger at the Goethe Institute in London. Neal, essentially sympathetic to reformist Communists of the Dubcek or Modrow sort, was someone whose fundamental sense of pattern and progress in history had been jolted by the speed and intensity of the change. Enzensberger's *Ach Europa!* brought a sense of involvement – however provisional – through the poetic qualities of insight, empathy, role-playing, parody: the material of culture, not the 'facts' of materialism. It was like watching a replay of the debate between Settembrini and Naphta in *The Magic Mountain*, with the German poet conjuring up magic which was the more powerful in its absence of system.

About political *solutions* Enzensberger was unforthcoming: about European unity pessimistic. His notion of the 'Italianisation of Europe' seemed to me to forbode the growing power of the Mafia, whose writ already ran unchallenged south of Rome, rather

than the combination of administrative chaos, economic shrewd-
ness and communal civility he (and most German intellectuals)
praised in Tuscany. There seemed no vehicle around to transform
this into a European politics. Carlyle's imagination made sense to
the Victorians because it created images and called for action, but
there was also a powerful state structure on the point of being
created, and reserves of labour and power whose achievements still
seem incredible today.

Charlotte Brontë took a chance and sent *Jane Eyre* off to a London publisher at the end of August 1847. It was a best-seller eight
weeks later. The railway on which she sent the MS hadn't existed
two years earlier. A system of 5,000 miles was laid down between
1845 and 1850, without concrete, dynamite, earth-movers, etc.
It has taken even the Germans nearly twenty years to build two
hundred miles of high-speed lines and Britain five to decide not to
build a high-speed link to the Channel Tunnel. Carlyle was more
effective than Marx and Engels because he had the imagination to
comprehend this power. He opened himself to the unexpected, the
irrational, the non-material – how men actually thought they acted;
how he felt when writing about them – he appealed directly to the
generation which had to control the market, or be destroyed by it.

Marx and Engels were essentially passive, believing that the tide
of economic change would carry their ideas to fulfilment. What
the 'hidden hand' of *laisser-faire* did in the previous generation,
dialectical materialism would do in theirs. Carlyle, on the other
hand, wrote to inspire an intervention in the social system akin
to that of the Evangelical revival in the religious sphere. And
to a remarkable extent he was successful. When a 'Marxist triumph' came about it was assisted by two vastly destructive wars
which derailed any logical development of capitalist industry and
greatly developed the powers of repression. Various states that
called themselves 'scientific socialist' took control over half the
world's population, but the corruption of power has taken its
toll; 'new socialist man' seeing his rulers wreck his life-chances
by their laziness, mediocrity and corruption, has – at least temporarily – abandoned this dream. Carlyle, on the other hand, with
his insistence on balancing the great impersonal forces against the
uniqueness and peculiarity of history, on the role of individuals
in historical change, and on analysing the physical and mental
processes of conveying information, seemed a prophet justified.

Carlyle stood for twenty years – between 1830 and 1850 – at the
point of interaction of an unprecedented number of disciplines. In
an odd way, this is paralleled today. Economics, politics, print-
capitalism, religion, poetry have again fused into the movements

which he would have recognised – in advance of practically all of his contemporaries – as altering totally the world in which he lived. His concepts – the 'cash-nexus', the 'mechanical age', the 'condition of England' – entered the national and indeed the European consciousness. His own politics ended in fulminating reaction, but his role in the politicising of English literature, through Disraeli, Dickens, Trollope and Meredith, and thus the creation of a British 'political culture', was incalculable.


## II


This isn't going to be a 'Carlyle and our times' anthology of the sort which used to infest second-hand bookshops' bargain trays, baffling people as to how this splenetic, dyspeptic reactionary ever managed to be significant. Even the creation of a vast mid-Atlantic exegetical industry still seems to have left him, as Engels put it, stranded by the tide of history. Yet his style – however violent, personal and uncouth – helped give British politics new autonomy and energy, and swung British social thought to German from classically-derived models, while his 'interdisciplinary' signifiers, derived from fashion and contemporary politics, seemed to make him truly the first post-modernist.

Take blue jeans. In explaining the collapse of the Communist order the words blue jeans came up as frequently as, say, Chernobyl or Solidarnosc. They were the easy symbol for what Eastern youth wanted: they incorporated American culture, sex, informality, classlessness, freedom. But the interesting thing was that, as the 1980s wore on, the image restructured itself. Denim became fashion. What had been the uniform of the drudges became the 'designer jeans' of the dandies, and started to project something quite different from the gentle pacifism of 1968. They appeared on scowling model-girls, all hips and padded shoulders, on their hunky studs, with two-day growths and the air of blackshirt hit-men of the 1920s: 'power-dressing' reflected fashion as international big business. By the time the refugees came through the unravelling curtain jeans were definable in terms of class: the Ossies wore the wrong sort, were 'instantly recognisable in their stone-washed jeans'. Albanians in their 'unfashionable flared nylon trousers' were the end. Indicative of a new confrontation which might have reassured him, this insight was beyond Marx. It would not have been beyond the author of *Sartor Resartus*.

Taken along with the reappearance on the political agenda of the matter of civil society, Carlyle gives the Scottish experience in the late eighteenth and early nineteenth century immediate relevance. He saw Europe in a *Zeitbruch* – what Saint-Simon called a 'critical period' – between two plateaus of more gradual development. With his background in Scotland – and the obvious influence of Ferguson – 'society' had to Carlyle a presence much more powerful and moulding than the atomism which Marx inherited from Adam Smith and Bentham. If its logic was more problematic, its resources in religion and social solidarity were much greater. So if his name recurs it is not for antiquarian or patriotic reasons: Carlyle broke off the 'matter of Scotland' dialogue in the early nineteenth century, but that dialogue was of much more than purely Scottish interest. Civil society is back on the agenda; 'the demon of mechanism' is smoking and thundering in far from metaphoric ways. Among the wealthy the 'monstrous ocean-moan of *ennui*' is as paralysing as it was in the 1830s. Outside the restaurant, in their 'rags and laughing savagery', the vast majority wait to break in.

## III

Reassessing Carlyle is also important in terms of Scottish history: because of the need to bridge the apparent chasm between the Enlightenment and the Renaissance of the 1920s – that century or more when the rest of Europe is reacting to industrialisation and nationalism while the Scots 'seem' to be plunged in a private and boring religious war. 'Seems' is important, for the more that we know about the real intellectual history of Victorian Scotland, the closer it lies – in the continuing importance it granted to 'society' – to the European main line than to that of England. The essentials of the English political structure were the strength of class – Dahrendorf's 'layer-cake of fine class distinctions' – the concentration of political activity in a highly-integrated and largely self-governing cultural/political elite, and the increasing concentration of politics in London. The fact that much of the elite was in origin Scots must not blind us to the fact that a distinct Scottish tradition continued. John Pocock and his colleagues have traced a discourse of 'civic humanism', concerned with the interactions of economy, ethics and society, from Machiavelli's historical studies to the pioneering sociology of Adam Ferguson, via George Buchanan and Samuel Rutherford's defence of Scottish constitutionalism against divine right theories of monarchy, and Andrew Fletcher's impassioned assault on metropolitan centralisation.

This concept of the small, knowable *polis* existing within loose structures of international agreement continued in Scotland in the nineteenth century, from the scepticism about parliamentary absolutism disclosed in the 'theoretical histories' of John Galt via the political theory of Chalmers' 'Godly Commonwealth' and the 'non-intrusionists' in the Kirk before the Disruption of 1843, to the ideas of the pioneer international lawyer James Lorimer, who argued for a united states of Europe as early as the 1880s. James Bryce, the historian of the Holy Roman Empire, applied an ideal of diffused sovereignty to proposals for Irish home rule and imperial federation in the 1880s, and during World War I became on the same grounds an advocate of the League of Nations. On the right F S Oliver, like Bryce an historian of America, campaigned for British federalism in the 1900s, while in a more inspirational way Allan Octavian Hume and Patrick Geddes helped mould the movement for Indian self-government.

The Scots tradition has retained both an European civic consciousness and something of the flexibility which was once supposed to inhere in the 'British way'. This has parallels with the 'self-government' tradition of Wales, and the inspiration it has provided for Leopold Kohr and his ideal of small-scale, environmentally-conscious society. It also belongs with the ideal of progress secured by conscious discussion now emerging in East Europe from the shadow of a decaying Marxian authoritarianism and a luridly-oversold *laisser-faire*. Marked by the words 'civic' and 'solidarity' this is 'civic virtue' in a new guise, something which can be transmitted to society in general through the education system and responsible popular media. Its essentials are the centrality of society, the non-absolute status of individuality and property, the importance of rules of conduct and social cooperation, a tolerance of and openness to religious belief, however unorthodox. This enables us to find possibilities of action which inhere within our own social experience. It also grants Scotland a peculiarly advantageous political position.

## Possibilities

### I

In *Latter-Day Pamphlets*, Carlyle's sourest and least ingratiating diatribe against his time, he let fly at George Hudson, the 'Railway King' of York, whose manipulation of the stock market at the height of the 'Railway Mania' in 1844–45 made him, temporarily, a power in the land. When the Mania ended, his mushroom schemes collapsed and he went into exile, like a Thackeray villain, in Boulogne. 'How much could one have wished that the making of our British railways had gone on with deliberation; that these great works had made themselves not in five years but in fifty-and-five!' Carlyle wrote when 'Suffrage' – public opinion – first lauded, then loathed, Hudson, for personifying its panic reaction. 'His worth, I take it, to English railways, much more to English men, will turn out to be extremely inconsiderable; to be incalculable damage, rather!'

Hudson at least got his railways built: During the period 1980-1990 billions of pounds surged into London office developments, often undertaken on giant rafts floated above decrepit railway stations. These provided accommodation for 1,600,000 office workers; most studies of the service sector, allowing for computerisation, expect their number to *decline* by 300,000. Railways are at least a form of transport. An empty office block is an empty office block. Environmental perils – dramatised by heatwaves, pollution, catastrophes of the Chernobyl sort – are now underlining the global crisis as obviously as cholera advertised urban congestion and lack of sanitation in the early nineteenth century. Yet fact and suffrage can still be ludicrously at odds, particularly in a state with a politics as dislocated as that of the United Kingdom, with its capacity to falsify political and economic priorities. Empty office blocks make – or made – sense in the 'casino capitalism' of Britain in the 1980s. Altogether elsewhere, the project of European unity is being undertaken at a period of industrial change as profound as that of the 1830s and 1840s, when the transport industries took over from textiles as the great motor of industrial development, a fact of which Britain's economic controllers are only – at best – fitfully aware.

## II

There are four differences from earlier phases of industrialisation. One: we cannot simply reduce our industrial commitments and painlessly move towards 'post-industry'. We have got so far up a particular, hazardous route that we have to evolve a type of 'super-industry' to get us back to safety: processes of manufacturing, transport and distribution in which new techniques of information and communications can make industry sensitive to global social and environmental requirements. In the long term this may lead to a planned 'de-industrialisation' – but not yet. Two, this process is not automatic: it will not be achieved by surrendering to market forces, but by the will to select priorities for concentrated research, development and financing. Three: if we fail to achieve this transition, this won't simply be a setback but will bring catastrophe to the present generation. Four: Britain may personify this crisis; it has no longer the resources or the will to overcome it.

Up to now this stark choice has been obscured by the survival of the old defence-based political order, and an over-centralised polity. This has been aggravated, in the United States and Great Britain, by the decay of politics as well as manufacture. A primitive and authoritarian informational system virtually destroyed the political/industrial system of the Communist world; an over-sophisticated system is sapping the English-speaking countries. 'Literature, too, has its Paternoster-row mechanism, its Trade-dinners, its editorial conclaves, and huge subterranean, puffing bellows;' wrote Carlyle in 1829, 'so that books are not only printed but, in a great measure written and sold, by machinery'. Widening the term, media management is now *itself* an industry, altering process, consumer and product. But it operates within its own closed-circuit, whose leading principles are short-term gain, not long-term development. Contrast the seriousness of the debate about politics in East Europe before the Communist system collapsed with the relentless triviality of the 'Western' values which have succeeded it.

What would Carlyle have made of the huge advances paid for Jeffrey Archer's pot-boilers? He would certainly have relished the fact that these gave him political significance, and aided the political career of his agent's husband, Dr David Owen. Or the rise to world significance of Robert Maxwell and Rupert Murdoch on the back of the headlong devaluation of British newspapers? Class politics of a restrictive, plebiscitary sort have been locked in place by the relentless triviality of a semi-literate press, reinforcing the difficulty of adapting the workforce to absorb – and originate – new ideas and innovations in industry, emphasising the 'rootlessness' of finance capital.

The reality of the Condition of England, however, *does* lie in the *Sun*, in the adverts for 'instant loans' that accompany the pin-ups and the loutish text. A glance at the *Financial Times* will confirm the impression of an overdrawn, undereducated, society. The domestic press may have to go through the rituals of party commitment, but the paper which used to be a solid prop of the Tory party, now printed in Frankfurt and Tokyo, has an international business clientele, and can spare no particular loyalty for the British Conservatives: if Britain is a bad investment, it will say so. The system into which it locks is no longer part of a national structure.

## III

West Germany personifies many of the positive aspects of the new industrial order, but it lacks the imagination, the sensitivity and – still – the reputation to 'sell' it. In the United Kingdom, by contrast, an extremely sophisticated information system was used to legitimise a government whose 'modernisation' efforts ranged from the inept to the disastrous, and which may have accomplished the destruction of the traditional British state system. The tale of Saatchi and Saatchi, which rose via the advertising campaign that hoisted Mrs Thatcher to power in 1979, and became the largest firm of its sort in the world, only to crumble when it moved into 'real' industry, seems emblematic. Advertising *coups*, anyway, confer a one-off advantage, after which the others catch up. Thatcherism may have been given its quietus by the selling of Jacques Delors' '1992', which took on enough momentum to ride out the contortions of the West and the startling alterations in the East. Those who rise by the ad, perish by the ad.

On the other hand, fate has set your man, like many another, crawling on the locks of this bloated, self-serving information economy, able to take advantage of its breakthroughs – faxing, cheaper phone calls, satellite TV, and a considerably expanded market for articles and programmes. It is always useful to be in the crows-nest, even if no-one below is paying attention, and one will have to take one's chance with the rest after the ship hits the reef. So . . .

## By Rocking-Chair through the Berlin Wall

### I

Graham Greene in his novel *It's a Battlefield* quoted Kinglake's *Crimean War* to the effect that if you were in the thick of a battle, and quite likely to be killed by it, you saw only a very small and possibly quite misleading part of the action. When the crowds were out on the streets of Leipzig or Prague, I was at home in Tübingen, watching them on television from my rocking chair. I felt rather like that Ronald Searle character who moved across the prairies of America and the steppes of Russia by the same means, encountering on the way every cliché known to the guide-books. Yet television and the German press brought me closer to the scene of the action than most British reporters who were on the spot, talking to the taxi-drivers or barmen, and making what they could of official briefings. Politics, now largely created by and 'aimed' at the media, had moved out to meet it. And, of course, unlike the British press, the German media stuck with it even after it had ceased to be 'hard' news. The 'qualities' continued to cover it in depth; the local papers related it to individual and community experience.

As a Scot, someone from an apparently unexcitable part of Europe far from the disturbances, I ought to have been marginal. Yet I found that my views were considered interesting, both in Scotland, where the media were trying to get direct access to reports from the continent, and in Germany, where the Scottish identification was a useful way of dissociating oneself from an unpopular British government. I was also, as a German speaker and resident, able to relate my own views to two societies of which I was a part – in conversations with academic and jour- nalist colleagues – an experience broadly similar to that of many 'Europeans'.

The scene I was reporting was of supra-national authorities simultaneously being created and destroyed; nationalities emerging and wilting. Suddenly one nineteenth-century super-state, Russia, seemed to follow another, the British Empire, into the shadows; even the United States itself seemed threatened – with Quebec likely to secede from Canada and English-speakers soon to become a minority in California. This was welcome. But appalling trans- national economic and environmental problems were also demand- ing that we spend the 1990s creating responsive and effective international bodies: something difficult to reconcile with tradi- tional notions of national sovereignty. Democratic freedoms in east Europe promised fundamental advance – nowhere had individual judgement and environmental integrity been subject to such sense- less handling – but the depressing histories of the 'succession states' of the Versailles treaty were already beginning to loom up: endemic economic problems, irresponsible elites, irridentism and racialism, with the arms dealers and the superpowers waiting offstage. The more our frame of reference is *ipso facto* multinational, the more we require our own *polis*, whether region, culture-nation or city- state: this was my ritual self-incantation. Was it justified? The above developments – and the likelihood of a British constitutional breakdown – may mean that Scotland emerges quite soon on the

European stage, but as something rather remote and, by the rest of Europe, rather unexpected (Wales, by contrast, scarcely a hundred miles from the Tunnel and the 'landbridge' to Ireland, is almost at the European 'core'). Ought we to be so marginal? I will argue here that the situation we are in can't be classified by present criteria, and isn't bound by European affairs. The Scottish experience *may* be as significant as in Carlyle's day. The 'secular' situation created by contemporary political and social trends, relates, now as then, to the recovery of a humanist discourse of social enquiry, political adaptation and international collaboration.

## Rumours of the Death of Marxism May Have Been Exaggerated

### I

Carlyle assaulted the complacency of *laisser-faire*: its a-historical bias, its assumption that its mechanical logic would convince on its own terms. This complacency marks the present situation in a Europe simultaneously subject to 'openings' and 'closures'. The fall of the command economies offers unprecedented prospects for 'orthodox' development; fearsome environmental threats demand not just the checking of orthodox technology, but in many cases its reversal. Surveying both tendencies in historical terms, democracy and market liberalism have turned out more marginal than the interpretation of a sympathetic press has insisted.

In fact the most plausible explanation of the East European break-up is, ironically, 'neo-Marxist'. American economic warfare, a 'post-Vietnam' manoeuvre designed to overextend Communist armaments while starving them of new technology, did what it was supposed to do. I was in at the beginning of this when I was a keynote speaker at the International Institute of Strategic Studies at Bruges in the autumn of 1977. There the talk was all about the deployment in Europe of new, sophisticated American nuclear missiles, supposedly to combat the enormous Russian superiority in conventional weapons. But a cool young man from the French ISS came out with the argument that the West overrated the Russians: 'If the Russians want to move their tanks across Poland, the Poles will stop them'. Far-fetched though this seemed in 1977, he was proved right two years later, when Polish Communism went into what proved a terminal crisis.

## II

The American strategy forced East Europe to concentrate on military re-equipment and advanced technology and sacrifice the modernisation of manufacturing industry, environmental protection, and consumer goods production. East Germany, as I found when I visited it in July 1990, was an object lesson in this collapse. It was a badly polluted and run-down society, but one where the black-red-white slogans that used to proclaim: 'The teaching of Marx is all-powerful because it is true', had ceased to count, along with 'real existing socialism', long before November 1989. The pretences of the party could only be kept up by privatising the satisfactions of its subjects. The DDR was neither socialist nor antisocialist; it was a-political. And from being a world-leader in the early 1970s in goods like machine-tools, it had lapsed into industrial obscurity.

There are proportionately more motorists in the DDR than in Scotland; per capita energy consumption in the DDR is 18% over the West German level, but there is scarcely a fifth of the number of telephones. The DDR reached a 1960s level of affluence, but the later stages of development – into information and conservation technology – simply failed to take off, and in fact receded as competition increased from the new industrial states of the Pacific rim. Moreover, the Honecker regime systematically marginalised anyone, such as Robert Havemann or Hans Modrow, who expressed any coherent socialist programme for remedying this situation, and Bonn's programme of 'buying the freedom' of dissidents gave it a permanent safety-valve.

Bonn in fact made the DDR into a Stalinist theme-park, a 'shadow-state'. Even at their worst, socialist dogmatics tend to build up the public at the expense of the private, and to exalt the common culture. But here the public and cultural sectors were run down, and the resulting *Spießbürgergesellschaft* – petty-bourgeois society – quickly affiliated itself to its western version, at the precise moment when America, Russia and Britain were all, economically, on the ropes. Reconstruction by Modrow-like reformers might have given the state some substance, and made incorporation difficult; Bonn's 'Deutschmark diplomacy' got the leaders it wanted, on its terms.

## III

This strategy seemed even more successful, from a German point of view, in that competitive rearmament and conservative economic policies also overextended and deformed the capital structures of the USA and Britain. From being the world's greatest creditor, with overseas balances of $141 billion in 1981, the United States had become by 1986 the world's greatest debtor, owing $261 billion. Moreover, domestically, the policies of two of the world's most reactionary governments concentrated wealth in an archaic metropolitan governing class, with a propensity to spend in a particularly bloated and tasteless way, rather than to undertake careful long-term industrial investment programmes.

The consequences of this were baleful for the two societies concerned, but multinationalism created a momentum, of innovation and consolidation, of its own – largely based on the paradigms of American firms. The revitalisation of the European ideal after 1980 was in great part due to displacement of a flagging elite of Eurocrats grouped round the old heavy industries and agriculture, by a new technocratic culture derived from the multinational firm. This saw a single European market not only as a logical development, but as the first stage in a new industrial revolution, based on the opening-up of the East European market. Hence the euphoria of the first Delors years in Brussels.

But the East European market foreseen was one which would have been subject to enlightened central control. Its progress would have been predictable: various forms of barter trade would have thrived. The more progressive East European states – East Germany, Czechoslovakia, Hungary – could fairly rapidly have been swung round to a form of social market; the others would follow more gradually. This did not happen. The collapse of Russian power was total; her shift to hard currency dealings brought down the whole existing structure of transfer payments; market economics, so far from being a tool for the empirical handling of the problem of adaptation, became an almost millennial panacea as the revelations grew of Communist indebtedness, incompetence and corruption.

All this time, West Germany was advancing to become the only world-class power in the EC. Although sustaining only 15% of EC population, she provided 40% of its manufacturing capacity, 40% of its exports and 33% of its internal trade. By 1987 Germany and Japan had become the effective paymasters of the old superpowers. In Paul Kennedy's evaluation, in which economic success preceded 'super-power' status, they were poised to become superpowers themselves. The problem was that his next stage, the overcommitment bugbear, promptly launched itself at the *Bundesrepublik* in 1990. Most German politicians would have settled for a confederal arrangement with a democratised DDR, by which the new government was given ten years to trade itself out of the mess the Communists had landed it in, subject to a much lower rate of exchange for the Ostmark, subsidies from the West, and freedom to restructure its economy in its own way.

Instead the coupling of fears that the *Bundesrepublik* would be invaded by millions from the East and that Gorbachev wouldn't survive in Russia, and the wholly unexpected victory of the eastern Christian Democrats in April 1990, forced the hastiest of marriages. With West Germany ceasing to be a controller, and becoming a participant, the prospect of measured change vanished, and with it much of the confidence the European elite had placed in the east as its new market. Democracy and the free market were no longer the instruments of adaptation to a rational multinational-dominated European order. They had taken on an alienated quality of their own: become a psychological liferaft to the multitudes gripped in the crisis.

## The Future Thatcher Lost

### I

British economic policy in the 1980s paralleled or even anticipated the Western decoupling of the traditional nation-state and the 'technostructure'. But instead of creating the new type of industry-facilitating order observable in West Europe, dogmatic *laisser-faire*, financial short-termism, and linkages to an internationalised, speculative capitalism put it beyond national control.

The British government was never silent about its libertarian mission, and many were Mrs Thatcher's 'photo-opportunities', basking in the adulation of Poles or Hungarians, but Britain's role in West Europe was obstructive, in East Europe unobtrusive, and overall in decay. Ultimately Britain – the *Sunday Times*'s 'declining second-rate power' – faces the prospect not just of economic and constitutional collapse, but of a final eviction from the 'high table': the seat in the Security Council, the membership of the Group of Eight, the headship of the Commonwealth. As the Cold War blocs break up, Britain's last token of great power status – her nuclear arsenal – is ceasing to count.

When I moved to Germany in May 1980, I did so with some apprehension. The UK's oil seemed to give it better chances for future development than Germany. Ten years on, with the pound down by 30% against the Deutschmark, 'radical' changes and 'reforms' (so flexible, these days, is political language) appear only to have intensified the British disease. Productivity has increased in manufacturing, but overall it is still scarcely half that of West Germany, while the manufacturing sector has, in relative terms, declined. Management and training are, even after ten years of aggressive rhetoric, still inferior. Research and development in non-defence sectors (and in particular in the vital environment sector) has declined in absolute terms. Employment looked good in the mid-1980s, but comparisons were distorted by the influx into West Germany from the East, and by cosmetic treatment of British statistics. Full-time jobs have been replaced by part-time, low-paid jobs, which now account for a third of the labour force. Inflation is more points above the European average than it was in the 1970s.

The consumption-led economic boom of 1986–88 reacted on the depleted manufacturing sector to produce a balance of payments deficit which amounted in 1990 to 4% of GNP; a circumstance in which the pound can only be protected by high interest rates which penalise capital investment and aggravate inflation. The savings ratio, increasing which was the central intention of the 'supply-side' economics adopted by this government, fell in 1989 to its lowest level ever. Even the budget surplus, acclaimed by the government as a major success, was achieved – and only for a time – by selling off public assets at knock-down valuations and reining back planning and investment in infrastructure, education and training, research, environmental improvement, and urban organisation.

The *economic* crisis has gone beyond the point at which it can be resolved by conventional party means. Achieved with the full co-operation of the financial world, the latter can be counted on to be hostile to any Labour government – even more hostile than the present City establishment, as it will be reinforced by an army of Conservative ex-ministers. At the same time such has been the social injustice inflicted by government legislation, that increased resistance to the power of a Labour-run state can be anticipated from trade unions and grass-roots organisations. Moreover, although the economy now seems beyond the control of the government, its 'economistic' assault on civil society and cultural life has been so deliberate a policy of cultural and ethical demoralisation that the qualities of resilience, communitarianism and voluntary effort which made Britain an innovative and humane society have been badly damaged.

To take one instance, from my own field. The bureaucratic rigidity of German *academia* could never have got the Open University, my old employer, up and running, yet the capacity for informal co-operation which made this possible has been choked off by the dogma of the 'bottom line'. A friend, applying for a chair in a Scottish university, found that the interview was about the financial management of the department, not with teaching or research. Small wonder that our universities, once the most innovative, are now the most demoralised in Europe. The concatenation of economic disorganisation and the subversion of civil society has induced a deadly solipsism, which is now destroying even those areas which the government regarded as its successes: the 'short-termism' and downright criminality of many in the financial world is marginalising the City of London as a financial centre, with Britain's 'invisible' trade account following manufacturing into deficit. Retailing, property, media and advertising – proclaimed as the great successes of the Thatcher epoch – have all seen 'limitless opportunity' lure them into deep financial difficulty.

When he came to Britain, in the 1880s, the American novelist Henry James remarked on the 'rottenness and *collapsibility*' of the governing class. That class surprised him, survived, and digested him. Could it recover again? The comparisons with conservative South Germany speak for themselves. To read the self-satisfied insularity of Roy Jenkins's *European Diary* – his obliviousness to any sort of activity which might be going on in industry, the British provinces, scientific or industrial research – is almost more depressing than studying the record of the last ten years. It is La Fontaine's fable of 'The Grasshopper and the Ant' all over again.

Mrs Thatcher embodied this predicament, a lethal amalgam of 'parliamentary sovereignty' and strong but confused convictions which subverted its conventions. Her transient political and economic successes became evangelical claims of moral rebirth. The dynamism continued even when the numbers went wrong. The fundamental economic problem remained, although old traditions – monarchy, deference, patriotism – were subverted by a new awareness of the politics and economics behind them. Instead a weird symbiosis between individualistic 'greed is good' radicalism and old-fashioned hedonism – the flight of 'serious money' into property and conspicuous consumption rather than industrial investment – split apart to disclose only the empty 'images' of public relations. When Mrs Thatcher tried to express her inner convictions, she only deformed Christian morality and Scottish Enlightenment thought into a primitive individualism. Launched at a mechanism as tradition-dependent as 'Britain', the result has been destructive in the extreme.

Could a Labour government repair this? The sort of centralisation practised by Mrs Thatcher appealed to some Labour party 'moderates', trying to clone replacements for such errant comrades as Woodrow Wyatt, Hugh Thomas and Bernard Ingham. 'All power is marvellous, absolute power is absolutely marvellous' *was* Mrs Thatcher: yet no-one, in the looking-glass world of Westminster politics, argued with the proposition. But a return to 1964, when Labour could back non-ideological 'modernisation', is scarcely possible. The economic situation is much worse. Manufacturing has contracted, and internationalised speculation in commodities, securities and currency has swollen grotesquely. The first was traditionally open to joint action with a Labour government. The second has no conceivable common interest with one. Such an administration might be allowed to pick up the tabs for the present government's excesses – just as the German general staff put the socialists into power to tidy up when they had lost World War I – but it is unlikely to be allowed to do anything remotely radical.

In 1945, and even in 1964, a substantial sector of British-owned industrial capital had an interest in promoting the welfare state, to maintain an adequately trained and disciplined labour force and a market for its products: as part of a corporate industrial society. Now that the ownership of capital and the organisation of industry have been internationalised, this motivation no longer operates. The commercial forces which backed Thatcher without qualification have done so because the City of London provides them with one of many suitable trading environments. Labour will look in vain for sustenance from this quarter, like the Mitterand government in France after 1981 – and *that* was in a country with a substantial industrial sector and a tradition of successful state involvement in the economy. Labour is still divided over defence and the absence of socialist objectives in Kinnock's programme. Should inflation produce union militancy, the stage might be set for a repetition of 1976, though in this case the EC, rather than the IMF, might provide the ambulance – at a cost.

## Common Sense and Scottish Prospects

I

The Thatcher episode has inflicted deep damage on relationships between the nations of the British Isles, which were always a rather odd combination of personal intimacy and cultural tension. The French political scientist Emile Boutmy wrote in the 1900s that the centralised state incorporated four nations which didn't like each other very much, something unusual in the context of France or Germany. If this was the situation when the Empire was still paying a high dividend, how much greater the tension today,when the 'British' connection has subjected Scotland and Wales to the rule of a party they did not elect and policies to which they remain implacably opposed.

This has expressed itself in the steady advance of support for independence and in enthusiasm for the ideal of Scotland in Europe: a proposition these days almost as popular as devolution. Yet Scotland hasn't passed through the experience of 'bourgeois regionalism' encountered elsewhere in Western Europe – in Catalonia, Baden-Württemberg or Lombardy. Rather the opposite. The independent Scottish business sector contracted during the 1980s with amazing speed. Baden-Württemberg has the headquarters of Daimler-Benz, a multinational with a turnover of £25 billion (about half the total Scottish GNP in 1987). Scotland's attempt to trade the autonomy of a local firm in return for the headquarters of Guinness ended in scandal and defeat: after all the trials and prison sentences, Distillers still went south.

The semi-autonomous Scottish administrative state was not primarily a mechanism for bourgeois economic development, but a means evolved after 1885 – when Scotland regained her cabinet minister and the Irish home rule crisis began – of cementing 'British' identity by offering problematic areas enhanced welfare rights. It wasn't coincidental that the Beveridge Report coincided with the greatest prestige of the Scottish Office under Tom Johnston. Nor that the capricious and opportunistic dismantling of the welfare state and the nationalised industries under Thatcher should have an earthquake-like effect on Scottish political allegiances.

The upshot has been a peculiar mixture of ill-temper and flippancy, observable on both sides. In England Conservative papers like the *Economist* and the *Sunday Times*, and authorities with some contact to Downing Street, such as Norman Stone, take a line of either 'Go away and don't bother us' or '*We*'ll go away and then you'll be sorry'. This has replaced the peculiar formulations by which Mrs Thatcher, erstwhile 'English nationalist', tried to contort herself into a Scots identity for visits north of the Border. Radical free-marketism could have taken 'bourgeois regionalist' initiatives. Michael Forsyth, no less, once came up with the notion of floating the Scottish £ against sterling (a proposal which bore the imprint of the cloven hoof of Michael Fry). But Thatcherism was as irrelevant to Scottish actuality as it was to European industrial change. It immolated the Scottish Conservative party on the pyre of the poll tax, and was thereafter put in isolation.

Scots hostility to London government, the City and the institutions of the English establishment has become such that 'Europeanism' now almost resembles a cargo-cult, an emotional resource, like supporting West Germany against England in the World Cup, which tallies imperfectly – to say the least – with vagueness about Scottish economic goals. In Wales Peter Walker eschewed confrontation and pursued a policy significantly different from Thatcherism. But he could use the Swansea-Newport corridor as an alternative development pole to South-East England – it was easier to reach Cardiff than Colchester from Heathrow.

Scotland doesn't have this option, and its development prospects have, in comparison with those of Wales, declined in the 1980s. Wales retains a heavy industry and manufacturing base – the coastal steelworks, the Ford and Bosch plants, and is close to the European core. The Ravenscraig closure and further contraction at plants like Howdens and Weirs could spell the end for the last of Scottish heavy industry. Strategic significance, that other and less welcome Scottish characteristic in the cold war years, is also on the wane. The Americans will withdraw from Holy Loch, the Admiralty from Rosyth. Armed forces reduction will curtail that disproportionate Scots participation revealed – quite unexpectedly – at the time of the Gulf War.

## II

We are placed in our present situation more by the 'Condition of England Question' than by our own economic evolution. As Neal Ascherson once pointed out, Scotland's place among the 'advanced' regions of Europe is uncertain. In certain respects, notably its banking and agriculture, it belongs among them; in others – in its political structure and urban life – it is more of a 'socialist state' than anything else to be found west of the Urals. It has been stuck in this distorting mould by its subordination to a British state, the power of whose conventions, bureaucracy and welfare institutions restricted the agenda of 'Scottish' politics.

In the late 1980s a fundamental withdrawal of consent to this system – dramatically evident in the response to the poll tax – has put Scotland through a process of 're-politicisation', like Hungary or Czechoslovakia. In this the role of the Scottish Constitutional Convention has been unusual and some respects revolutionary. Before 1988 Labour had pronounced itself reluctant to abandon the 'leading role' which had given it such an overwhelming dominance of the politics of West Central Scotland. By accepting proportional representation in the Convention, not to speak of other proposals for the representation of women and minorities, it has done so. This has had two effects, both with their East European parallels. The pluralistic structures now being considered can release new imagination and potential for social co-operation. More negatively, the adaptation of areas of the welfare state into a more market-structured situation could see the old *nomenklatura* turn into the new capitalists.

'Bourgeois regionalist' movements in Europe have about them a strong sense of exclusivity among the already privileged. Perhaps the most effective of them has been the Conservative distortion of the government of Britain into promotion of South-East England, Nimbya, the land of Essex Man. The politicisation of other, under-privileged regions – Corsica, Ulster, Euskadi – has become locked in communal tension and violence. The pacific and deliberative Scots experience has often seemed to us tediously low-key. If successful, however, it could act as a model. But it must develop by widening its agenda to consider what Scotland's function will be in the British Isles and in Europe.

On one hand the coincidence of British economic collapse with the achievement of the European project suggests that Britain might 'implode' into the European community. This would be no bad thing: a Britain which perceived *all* its possibilities in European politics might give European institutions a flexibility and effective-ness, presently lacking, which could accelerate the integration of the other powers, especially Germany. The *quid pro quos* might be substantial. European control of arterial transport routes – main railways, airports and motorways – could secure rapid communica-tions without wasteful competition and overinvestment. Ulster or Hong Kong could prove more tractable as 'European' problems. 'These islands', as the Irish put it, could become a useful prototype for the environmentally-based supra-regional grouping which must evolve within the new Europe.

If the inadequacies of 'Britain' deposit Scotland and Wales in Europe, it will be a Europe which secular economic change and a decade of Thatcherite abstention have made a 'Greater German co-prosperity sphere'. But exploration of the history of the continent's major power, Germany, may also disclose some habitable interstices.

## Rifkind Redux

### I

Politicians, as a tribe, are not much approved of by the public. When we put *Grasping the Thistle* together for the BBC at the end of 1986, a specially commissioned opinion poll revealed that they were valued way below ministers or journalists, or even town councillors. One of the standard arguments against devolution is that it will simply expand their numbers: whoever manages it will be the man who introduced cuddly rabbits into Australia.

The popularity of individual politicians soars and slides vertiginously. Margaret Thatcher was magic one year, rubbish the next, although she seemed to remain appallingly consistent throughout. For a few dizzy days John Major was the greatest statesman who has ever lived, before the Great British Public reckoned he wasn't really up to much. In November 1990 130,000 turned out in Erfurt to cheer Helmut Kohl, bawling optimistic platitudes about making East Germany a blossoming garden; in April 1991, when he made his next trip, only 600 bothered to come out and boo. There is a change here – a disturbing one – from the veneration once granted, over scores of years, to Gladstone or Lloyd George. Both were supremely devious customers, but they interacted in some symbiotic manner with the beliefs and ideals of their supporters.

The receding tide of confidence is visible throughout Europe, despite a greater involvement of the people in public affairs, through proportional representation and state-funded political parties. In Germany the percentage voting, traditionally high, is declining to 'British' levels – around 70%. The Italian Communists – long the 'clean men' of Italian politics – have fled from the name to which Gramsci, Berlinguer and Visconti gave their allegiance. Christian Democracy in many areas is in the hands of the Mob. Spain's Socialists have run into increasing scandals, and the rule of Mitterand has the echo of Baldwin: 'He did not care in which direction the car was travelling, as long as he sat in the driver's seat'. Yugoslavia, once the hope of the left through its self-management schemes, has collapsed into civil war.

One consequence of the exhaustion of parliamentary politics is that loyalty is transferred to symbolic leaders. Not just – or even in the first line – the royals or the pope. The boulevard press has left its mark on both. But presidents, once elderly academics and ex-ministers, now incorporate vague but powerful social ideals: no way are Vaclav Havel, Lech Walesa or Mary Robinson figureheads. Another, much more sinister, is the rise of xenophobic movements.

Some are nationalistic, like the German Republikaner, the Austrian FPÖ and the French Front National, with enough veterans of the old Right capering about to put most people off. Others are a more ambiguous projection of bourgeois regionalism, such as the Italian Lega Lombarda, constructive in its federalism and commitment to regional planning and environment issues, but also drawing on prejudice against immigrants and the 'poor South'.

What Richard Crossman called 'the charm of politics' seems to be weakening. This is visible even in the new generation in the German SPD. Oskar Lafontaine and his – my – contemporaries are an attractive and civilised lot, but somehow don't project themselves much above *Land* level; while an old monster like Helmut Schmidt, with his depressions and foul temper, was never less than interesting. Helmut Kohl and his friends in the conservative CDU literally have no successors; opinion about the Free Democrats is summed up by the amiable slogan which followed their ditching of the social-liberal coalition in 1982 – 'Give opportunism a chance – vote FDP', and the less said about the Greens during their eight years in Bonn, the better. Their professed pacifism allowed an internal politics which would have done credit to the last days of Robespierre. One senses that the compulsion to make democracy work, which filled German politics after the awful interregnum of 1933–45, has departed.

## II

1980s Britain, of course, had political personality in abundance and was thoroughly glad to get rid of her in 1990. But the point about Thatcher was that she was *against* politics: theoretically, she wanted the whole business surrendered to the invisible hand of the market, or Lord Hanson, or whatever. She was a Conservative of average abilities who swung herself into prominence by endorsing the fantasies of businessmen and publicists who salivated at the power that she offered them. Her own party reacted pliably: no-one more so than Malcolm Rifkind, Secretary of State for Scotland.

Rifkind and I had coincided at Edinburgh University as presidents of our respective political clubs, but when interviewing him all I could really pin down was an early taste for double-breasted suits (which *virtually the whole international political community* was wearing a year or so later). He had his disadvantages as a performer. 'What I hadn't been prepared for,' I wrote in my diary, 'is how frightening Rifkind is as a speaker. The voice is well-projected, but the face seems to have an independent life, with staring eyes which outBenn Benn and a visor-like smile whose effect is appalling.' Still, I was intrigued by him, because most of the livelier Scottish entrepreneurs – Forte, Wolfson, Stakis, Okhai – were 'two-culture' men, and success in Europe would require such qualities. Perhaps he had them. There was a rumour that Harold Macmillan had remarked, after an early Rifkind speech, that here was a new Disraeli. He had made a good impact both at the Scottish Office as junior minister and at the Foreign Office after 1983. His duels with Donald Dewar were reckoned a cut above the usual Commons level. I find from my diary that I seconded the notion of a potential Disraeli, or at any rate another Walter Elliot.

I also noted that effective leadership required some sort of intellectual *entourage*, something not conspicuous around any of the Scottish political leaders. Why didn't this develop? Instead a meek ambition accommodated itself to the requirements of his leader, only to be further imposed on by ideological demands which led to a bizarre sequence of events in 1990 when Rifkind had to see off the intrusion into Scottish politics of the Downing Street-approved Michael Forsyth and his extraordinary menagerie of advisers. This episode concluded with the, by all accounts pivotal, role played by Rifkind in the fall of Thatcher. If, indeed, the situation was that she would have beaten Heseltine on a second ballot – the constituency party activists would have seen to that – but the prospect so terrified the Cabinet that they decided to push her over while she was still groggy from the first shock, then Rifkind handled his dagger with skill. He escaped from the Scottish Office to another ministry, which is rare enough, but he did not leave Scottish Toryism healthier than he had found it.

## III

There was nothing flashy about Rifkind, while a stock exchange ambience always hovered about Peter Walker, his Welsh opposite number, and the latter's renewed interest in family life was implausible even by Tory party standards. But Walker threw himself into Welsh affairs, listened, helped, co-operated with his political opponents, and made Wales an altogether more hopeful place by the time he left. Much the same went for his partner Lothar Späth in Baden-Württemberg, whose exit was altogether more sulphurous. Yet I'm quite proud of having my professorial appointment signed by Lothar Späth, despite the fact that some of his Cabinet appointments were even more right-wing than the Thatcherites, and caused me personal difficulty through their conservatism.

Rifkind denied it in interview, but he tried to run Scotland as a crown colony. This was difficult enough anyway, particularly for a professional man who lacked the business connections that George Younger, and most of his predecessors in the Scottish Office, had relied on. It was next to impossible with a party as moribund as his. The poll tax was pushed through, quangos stuffed with nonentities, the Scottish Development Agency demoralised, Newbattle Abbey College closed down. When he tried to remonstrate with international big business and its 'rationalisation' plans – with Caterpillar or British Steel – he was politely told to get stuffed. He could have made trouble: his only rival among the Scottish Tories was the impossibly devolutionist Alick Buchanan-Smith. He could have started some sort of dialogue with people in Scotland who had ideas. But the impression he always gave was of someone socially isolated, intellectually indifferent, constrained by the political game. The two-culture man was not enlarged by his politics. Instead one seemed to see, on Thatcher's part, the traditional ploy of the despot: use servants from minorities; they are easier to blame and dismiss.

Rifkind still saw himself in high politics, still believed that these had a meaning. Scotland was the necessary endurance test, to be managed discreetly. And what was the ultimate goal? The obstacle race to Downing Street, the bank directorship in the City? I do Rifkind the credit of thinking it to be the former. But the sad thing was the lack of imagination he demonstrated. Hamish Henderson once recollected how as a schoolboy – and a member of the Young Communist League – he had recognised Walter Elliot while the latter was visiting the Paris Exhibition of 1937. Elliot had given him lunch, and launched, *inter alia*, into a critique of Hugh MacDiarmid's fascist leanings. 'Wait and see what we do next year in Glasgow' had been his parting shot. And the Glasgow Empire Exhibition was an apt *finale* to a short but constructive spell at the Scottish Office. By contrast Rifkind never went beyond the defensive.

The whole thing must have seemed unimaginably tedious. Endless hours in planes and sleepers, no real initiative possible, lowly status in cabinet: 'eyeless in Gaza, at the mill with slaves'. As time went on, Rifkind seemed more shackled than culpable, with ultimately nothing to show for his stewardship: the poll tax abandoned, the local authorities still confident; the Thatcherites vengeful, the opposition unimpressed. 'What does it matter who sits in parliament', Trollope makes Phineas Finn say in *Phineas Redux*, 'The fight goes on just the same. The same falsehoods are acted. The same mock truths are spoken. The same wrong reasons are given. The same personal motives are at work.' Phineas ends up successful but somehow empty, his real politics buried in his native Ireland. Contemplating Rifkind, one has the same sense of a good man wasted by a bad system.

In the 1980s Scotland underwent cultural developments in many ways as dramatic as those which changed Irish culture in the 1890s. Then the Irish Chief Secretary, Gerald Balfour, a Unionist, won sympathy as an institutional moderniser and cultural patron. The verdict on Rifkind was symbolised by an odd incident in the last months of his term of office. With the death of his widow Valda in 1989, the cottage of Hugh MacDiarmid at Brownsbank near Biggar became tenantless, and George Galloway MP raised the question of preserving it as a memorial in a letter to the Secretary of State. He received a reply from the office of Ian Lang, the housing minister, thanking him for drawing Mr MacDiarmid's housing problems to his attention, and saying that the Minister would give these due consideration . . .

# 2  Two Cheers for Germany

## On the Balance

'One is certain of nothing but the truth of one's own emotions.' . . . It was not an original remark, nor had Frieda appropriated it passionately, for she had a patriotic rather than a philosophical mind . . . It betrayed that interest in the universal that the average Teuton possesses and the average Englishman does not. It was, however illogical, the good, the beautiful, the true, as opposed to the respectable, the pretty, the adequate. It was a landscape of Böcklin's beside a landscape of Leader's, strident and ill-considered, but quivering into supernatural life.

E M Forster, *Howards End*

I

At the end of February 1991 I found myself contemplating my fourth conference on European regionalism in as many months. We had discussed regionalism where the breakers surged down on the strand of Cardigan Bay at Coleg Harlech; under the near-vertical cliffs of the Danube valley at Blaubeuren; above the pines of the Schwarzwald at Freudenstadt; in a snowstorm on the Alphaville campus of the Ruhr-University at Bochum. We had discussed regionalism with Catalans, Poles, East Germans, Austrians, Irish, Welsh, Swedes and Czechs. Now a further colloquium was scheduled for Bonn in May and for Glasgow at the beginning of 1992. At all these meetings the problem was to put a curb on the imaginations of politicians and businessmen, students and trade unionists; region was speaking cooperation as well as peace unto region.

But over these discussions had loomed the war-clouds of the Persian Gulf. At Freudenstadt B52s were flying 30,000 feet above us loaded with bombs; by the time we assembled at Bochum more high explosive had been dropped on Iraq and Kuwait than had been dropped on the Ruhr in World War II. American super-dreadnoughts – half-century old marine dinosaurs – were hurling one-ton shells at the troops of Saddam Hussein, and conservative regimes in both the USA and Britain, whose economic competence had been abysmal, were leading in the polls. If it was encouraging to find a reunited Germany underplaying its national identity, it was dismaying to find that the ghosts of Clausewitz and Bismarck had successfully transferred their residence elsewhere.

In early 1991 Europe's rich uncle – in its inadequacies as well as its successes – was engaged in morbid self-examination. Its exporting success had rebounded. German firms had been found supplying submarine plans to South Africa and poison gas plants to Libya and Iraq. Its long pacifist tradition ran into dispute. Did those kids on demonstrations, in their Arab headgear, realise what their grandparents had done to the Jews? According to Paul Kennedy, great powers rise because they are economically strong; they then fall through political and diplomatic overcommitment. In 1991, thanks to the skill of its foreign minister, Hans-Dietrich Genscher, Germany stood on the edge of being a great power. But its reluctance to become one, instead seeing its future within a united Europe, won it few plaudits.

## II

As far as Scotland – and in the case of my own patch, Baden-Württemberg, its partner-region Wales – was concerned, Germany had to be reckoned with. Its unity and its Europeanism coincided with the precipitate decline of the centralised British state that had entrapped them. For the second of the Conservative ministry's two wars, the hat had to be passed round. The decay was patent, occasioned not just by military over-commitment, but by the peculiar ineptitudes and misinterpretations of the Thatcher years. In 1989 France, or rather Paris (decentralisation seemed to have been told to get lost) grabbed the limelight in the grand manner for the bicentennial of its revolution, and kept it until revolutionary reality caught up with celebration. The East European upheavals seemed to be triggered by the bicentennial, but were modest in comparison with Paris's vast new buildings and endless parades. West Germany was almost apologetic about its triumph – 'Can we cheer now?' seemed to be the feeling in Berlin as the Wall fell. Britain reacted ineptly, setting in motion the sequence of events – from Nicholas Ridley expressing himself like a golf club bore after his fourth whisky, via a Chequers conference on 'the German character' minuted with crass insensitivity – which evicted a ruling premier: something unique in peacetime Britain. Mrs Thatcher's durability and high profile had masked a spectacular collapse in Britain's international role, her 'revival' no more than hiccup in a process of overall decline. The European Community matured; the Cold War weakened; Thatcher failed to cope with both.

There *was* a period of Thatcher ascendancy, between 1984 and 1987. Mitterand and Chirac were *cohabiting* – which sounds more fun than it turned out to be, and Helmut Kohl bumbled through a series of domestic crises, with a torpid economy. Thatcher had beaten the Argentinians and the miners, inaugurated an economic boom, and enjoyed the success of her first privatisations: endlessly ascending share prices guaranteeing fat profits for the punters who got theirs at a discount. American investors, deploying the surpluses that Reagan's taxation 'reforms' had handed them, and quitting manufacturing for globalised securities trading in communications and services, noisily applauded. Compared with preoccupied Europeans, and bemused old men in the White House and the Kremlin, Thatcher seemed dynamic and in control of new capitalist techniques. She knew how to use publicity, and discovered the Russian *dauphin* Gorbachev, who needed to know how to use it. When Chernenko helpfully died (how could they tell?) while Gorbachev was in Britain – in fact in Edinburgh – Thatcher was *in situ* as his 'honest broker' with the United States. Until Ronald Reagan had learned his new script, she *was* the voice of the West. But by late 1987, with the stock-market crash, she ran into trouble. The Single European Act, Jacques Delors' script for 1992 – substantially drafted by her former trusty, Lord Cockfield – made the principle of deregulation acceptable in Europe, but left her looking eccentrically nationalist. The European tendency was to restructure public intervention, not to abolish it: to reduce it in commerce but enhance it in research and development, transport and the environment. Britain's underfunded and demoralised universities, her archaic and dangerous road and rail systems, and her polluted water supplies set no example to anyone in the battle to establish an adequate infrastructure for a united Europe.

The salience of nuclear disarmament, in a Europe no longer ideologically divided, undermined Britain's last claims to world power. Nuclear weapons had always been an appalling drain on national investment, yet Thatcher could not use her nuclear status to force Kohl in 1988 to accept new missiles, and Bush slapped her down as sharply as Dulles had Eden at the time of Suez. Deutschmarks mattered more than British hydrogen bombs. Thatcher at Bruges in

1988 – opposing European monetary and federal union – sounded defiant but masked weakness and indecision. The City, sustained by speculation in vast currency flows and continually-fluctuating currency levels, would be hit by the managed currency of the EMS, but the amorality of its establishment was a big enough gift to its European rivals. Sir Alan Walters wanted Downing Street to locate the City in an Atlantic rather than a European future, but the 'special relationship' was no healthier than the FT Index. Airstrip One – all Thatcher had on offer – was a depreciating asset.

The economic leadership of Europe had long since been forfeited. Britain was now fighting it out with other low wage/low productivity economies like Spain and Portugal as a site for Japanese and American branch plants. The Falklands campaign wiped out British influence in South America. Thatcher on South Africa did ditto for the Commonwealth, while Far Eastern relationships were complicated by the fact that the Chinese had turned out far nastier than the Russians were supposed to be: inconvenient for the future of Hong Kong. By the time she fell, she was barely talking to Gorbachev, let alone 'doing business' with him. When the British rapidly endorsed American strategy in the Gulf, the reasons were all too patent – six years of oil reserves at present rates of extraction in the North Sea, nine in America. None of the above were signs of strength.

The suspicion could never completely be avoided that Thatcher's opposition to any scheme of self-government for Scotland was rooted in the conviction, first that this would be the slippery slope, second that the terminus of that slope, Scottish independence, would result in Britain's eviction from the remaining niches she occupied as a 'great power'. Yet, as the European Communities' power grows, and London, Brussels and Paris become only three hours distant by train, traditional diplomacy will give way to regional input into Community decision-making and subject-based collaboration, most notably in third-world development and environmental issues. The need for direct representation in Brussels and elsewhere of the various national and regional components of the British Isles will grow. And one British contribution, throttled under Thatcher, could give a European foreign policy a unique strength – the cultural linkages built up by the Commonwealth.

In foreign affairs, as elsewhere, Mrs Thatcher was dynamic, insensitive, and to the old order disastrous. The diaries of Roy Jenkins show the assumptions of the von Papens who saw her as a necessary corrective whom they could still keep in check. Instead she smashed through the crumbling fabric of Churchillian Britain and disappeared in the dust and rubble, leaving practically nothing behind that any 'moderate' successor could build on. The Gulf notwithstanding, Britain is either down there with the Spaniards and the Canadians, or can dissolve itself into a new Europe. Since this will be based on the regions and imply a benign role in international development, the transition will not be easy.

## Super-Industry

### I

At present, it is not even being attempted. A post-Thatcherite cabinet, purged of toadies and authoritarians, retains the momentum of centralisation. Local government after the replacement of the poll tax will be weak local government, while business leaders continue to moan about the damage any devolution of power (along lines utterly orthodox on the continent) will do to them. Meanwhile, the elaborate post-modernist towers of the City of London rise, monuments to the 'enterprise' of a panic flight of capital from equities to property after the crash of October 1987. Will they ever be tenanted?

Not if the case histories of some Thatcher success stories are anything to go by. Saatchi and Saatchi's stock market valuation was 700p a share in 1987, and the brothers were rumoured to be bidding for nothing less than the Midland Bank. By late 1990 their shares were worth less than 40p. Image-making, as much as the hocus-pocus of 'financial services', had suffered a stunning collapse, and other stories from the City – Polly Peck, Brent Walker – made the business practices of Dickens' Merdle and Trollope's Melmotte seem strait-laced.

In the mid-1980s Germany's concentration on manufacturing was branded as eccentric. World economies were supposedly moving towards the service industries. This Anglo-American line was ideological and opportunist. The service sector had internal differences – between fast food and computer programming – far greater than those separating it from manufacturing industry, but it was open to manipulations which made it seem to pay. The financial pages of German newspapers are to do with making things: firms (scarcely ever threatened by takeovers) being assessed by research, innovation, productivity and market share, etc, with helpful little diagrams to explain these to the lay public. In Britain the equivalent yardstick was making money – by share value appreciation or dividends – with few questions asked about how. As a result the

USA and Britain found themselves after 1987 in a *cul-de-sac*, with swollen low-productivity service-industry sectors, a financial sector which had decoupled from manufacture, and an involvement in third-world debt which penalised the world's poorest countries.

But image and reality radically diverged. To young and ingenuous East European advocates of the free market such actualities were outperformed by simplistic Anglo-Saxon attitudes. West Germany gave reform movements in East Europe their visible symbol of economic success, what the Britain of Cobden and Bright had been to the liberals of the 'Vormärz'. But the models of Balczerowicz and Klaus were quite different from the 'social market', with its mixture of state-sponsored technological innovation, long-term indicative planning and social corporatism. The 'social' element in the 'social market' is substantial: *Die Zeit* in July 1990 estimated subventions and protection measures as affecting over 50% of West German GNP. This is an index of an altogether different economic politics.

In 1988 I ran into a policy-maker from the Department of Employment in Bamberg. She had been seconded to the *Bundesanstalt für Arbeit* (Federal Labour Office) in Nürnberg and marvelled at the long-term approach the Anstalt took to a forthcoming reform of the Federal Pensions Law. In Britain, by contrast, the business of a policy unit was to supply, at three weeks' notice, the minister – then Lord Young – with a plausible parliamentary answer. This consultation is inevitably a burden on production, like the high wages, long holidays and short hours of the German labour force. The compensation is the high degree of adaptability which stems from 'social partnership' and 'solidarity'.

This 'corporate' approach means long lead-in times for social and technical innovations. To cite two examples from transport. The express railways which opened in 1991 were part of a programme set in motion in the early 1970s when most governments saw transport solutions as more cars on more roads. The evolution of the 'Inter-City Express' programme reflected the rigidities of the German approach, but produced a system for effective volume pro-duction. Just in time. 'Traffic thrombosis' has made most German urban areas create 'transport associations' with 'heavy' suburban *S-Bahn* trains and tramways – usually upgraded to 'metros' or 'urban railways' – for the main flows, and buses for the suburbs. This involved technology, social planning, market research, architecture and design, as well as economics. The result is a system which can be applied country-wide and organised for export: not unique to Germany, but far different from anything existing in Britain, where a piecemeal approach, dogmatic privatisation and underinvestment has produced the transport chaos of London.

## II

Where does this innovative spirit and work-ethic come from? One explanation is unappetising: the *German* worker is highly paid and highly skilled; but routine labour comes from *Gastarbeiter* – Italians, Spaniards, Turks, Greeks and Jugoslavs – who have lower wages, little job security, and no civic presence whatever. (Most Germans are against giving them even limited political rights.) Innovation is always welcome to the skilled, Carlyle's 'chief body-servants of the Steam engine', the installers and maintainers of new technology. Its victims, the unskilled, disappear from the class equation. Still, *Gastarbeiter* wages are well over the British norm, and despite high wages *Standort Deutschland* (manufacturing in Germany) pays well enough to keep 38% of GDP (against 25% in Britain) in manufacturing.

The reasons for success lie in a three main factors: finance is committed to industry; workers are highly-trained and involved in the strategy of firms; and the culture is egalitarian and work- rather than expenditure-governed.

Underlying the first two is the key notion of social partnership. The German banking system is complex and rooted in the community, whether through the *Kreissparkasse* or 'county savings banks' or the union-owned *Bank für Gemeinwirtschaft* or 'Community Enterprise Bank'. As a non-house owning society, people's savings have gone into industrial enterprise. The crucial linkage in British politics – between mortgage rates and electoral success – would leave the Germans baffled. The big banks – and there are, effectively, only three – have since the 1880s closely involved themselves with the strategic decisions of manufacturing industry, and have been prepared to forego immediate profit for long-term success.

Thatcher's 'success' in cutting down union power was perhaps as illusory as the apparent union hegemony in the 1970s. A badly-led and worse-informed movement, too much influenced by old demarcation disputes, 'uninvolved' unskilled workers, political ideologues and sheer inertia, made little contribution towards industrial modernisation or social equality, let alone any future socialist strategy. When Len Murray and a TUC delegation visited the Open University in the mid-1970s, they seemed devoid of any concept of working-class education, had nothing to say to the academics, and could make nothing of the proposals for distance learning courses in politics, union organisation and social policy that were put to them.

But was the 'collapse' of union power under pressure of mounting unemployment in the 1980s a reality? There was little real transfer of power to a management which remained poor by European standards; government succeeded – for a time – in using unemployment to restrain wage inflation but real wages continued to rise while productivity remained comparatively static and low. Union rationalisation and mergers occurred for political rather than economic reasons, and resulted in eccentric entities like the General Municipal and Boilermakers' Union. Against this the DGB (German Trade Union Confederation) is not only organised on logical industrial lines, but maintains an extensive research, regional and educational structure of a type which the Welsh or Scottish TUCs would regard as a model. Most DGB activists are aligned with the SPD, but the two are quite independent of one another and some DGB leaders are in the CDU – as real representatives of organised labour and not the outrageous menagerie of Conservative trade unionists in Britain. This confirms the situation of the two *Volksparteien* in the political centre and the union movement, as a component of this, is recognised by the establishment, through Presidential and Prime-Ministerial visits and addresses. This contrasts with the contempt with which Thatcher treated the TUC. Recognition breeds respect, and although not all the DGB's 'community-useful' enterprises have won plaudits (in the 1980s the careers of the trade union-owned Neue Heimat building firm and the Co-op ended in painful financial scandals) the unions have played a major role in keeping Germany a manufacturing country, carefully distanced from the lure of 'financial services'.

The final point is that German industrial leaders live modestly. The salary of Karl-Otto Pohl, former head of the Bundesbank and the 'banker's banker', was DM 600,000 a year (£200,000). That of Iain Vallance, executive chairman of British Telecom, is over £500,000. Few people in Germany would grudge Pohl his salary – 'Er hat es gut verdient' ('He's worked for it') – I doubt whether many would say the same of a man whose firm rips a 60% profit off every long distance call . . .

## III

German industrial co-ordination has much to do with a political order which promotes economic and fiscal stability, and decentralisation in decision-making. The 'independence' of the

Bundesbank is frequently cited as a ground for privatising the Bank of England, but stems from its being jointly owned by the Banks of the separate *Länder*, as part of the federal constitution. Federalism was reluctantly accepted by the Germans after World War II. Both the socialist and the 'national-conservative' traditions were against it. But it has since steadily increased in popularity, to around 70% approval. In the 1970s the Social-Liberal coalition of Willy Brandt and Helmut Schmidt trenched on the powers of the *Länder* in the interests of social equality, but under the looser rein of Helmut Kohl, Germany has for the last ten years been increasingly subject to centrifugal forces which have renewed initiative in the *Länder*, and stimulated collaboration with other European regions.

What has been the 'secret' of the 'effective part' of the German constitution? We try, going out from Bagehot, to detect an equivalent of Westminster and Whitehall, but although we find a replication of British parliamentarianism, it works through a mechanism of federalism and a simple form of proportional representation (the constituency and list system). The key to it – and in part to the German 'problem' – lies in the 'mix' between civil society and the state.

The Germans derived the principle of *Selbstverwaltung* (local self-government) from the British. By this *we* understand a form of 'devolution by profession or convention', whereby lawyers and doctors run their own professions. The Germans took over the rhetoric, but decentralised the formal power of the state. The decentralist *tradition* in Germany can be overdone. The imperial *Ritterschaften* and the free towns were hit by the Reformation and the horrors of the Thirty Years' War. There was no wealthy Whig nobility and substantial tenant-farmer class to establish an 'interest' in running local government. The peasantry kept its head down, until sovereigns – and Napoleon – disrupted the old structures in favour of agricultural modernisation and a secular bureaucracy, legal reform, and uniform church-state relations.

This local level of the state, determined by an accumulation of administrative laws from all epochs of modern German history – including 1933–45 – is very solid. I pay my income tax to the local authority (which retains roughly 15% of it, the rest being divided equally between *Bund* and *Land*). The local state is thus strengthened from the ground up, but it has a structure – of government and bureaucracy – broadly similar throughout Germany. The rights of the citizens are entrenched, and the British government's assaults on local autonomy would not be tolerated.The German bureaucracy is decentralised: at every level of elective government the relevant office of central government is 'across the road'.

As to the effects? Take Baden-Württemberg, Wales' partner in European high-tech development. Like Wales, Baden-Württemberg has much hilly, unproductive, land. Unlike Wales, it has no coal, no copper or slate and no tradition of large-scale industry before the late nineteenth century. Yet since the war the *Land* has come to dominate European industry. Its own firms – Bosch, Porsche, Zeiss, and above all Daimler-Benz – are major multi-national players. It has secured the high-value-added operations – research, product developing and marketing – of existing multi-nationals such as IBM and Kodak. It has used state action to influence sub-contracting policy in favour of locally-owned small firms. Its 'technology-transfer' arrangements, innovation centres located in technical universities and colleges, have put innovation in the public domain – as a raw material for general industrial modernisation, not as the possession of the big players.

Lothar Späth, state premier in Stuttgart until 1991, presided over the political-industrial complex of the 'Neckarmetropole' and early in the 1980s preached the coming of the 'Europe of the Regions'. But Baden-Württemberg isn't a typical region: it may pose more of a problem than a solution. It benefitted from the westward migration of firms and two million individuals after World War II, and it concentrated the leading hi-tech producers to a degree which has decreased the possibility of other regions acquiring such high-value operations. Without effective infrastructural planning policies, this has produced an alarming level of congestion and pollution in the north of the *Land*. More generally, Germany is suffering the physical consequence of 15% of Europe's population producing 40% of its manufactured goods. Baden-Württemberg literally *works*, but is it a one-off success in a zero-sum game?

## Grandeurs and Miseries of the Language

### I

Rubbish TV is usually assumed to be international: on satellite, endless supplies of American soaps, Japanese computerised cartoons, and those semi-pornographic but depressingly hygienic Eurogames like *Tutti Frutti* which are as close as the continent comes to the glories of the British popular press. But every so often I switch the box on and see something like: Two very fat young men, resembling Disney's little pigs, and dressed in white Tyrolean outfits, are singing into short but rather suggestive looking transmitter mikes. They are singing about home, mountains, girls and Yodel-ee-hi-ho. In front of them in a vast modern hall rank upon rank of bald male and blue-rinse female heads are swaying in rhythm, left-right, left-right. Seen close up, no single face appears under sixty, attractive or in any way even individual. The effect echoes George Eliot's remark in her essay on the German peasantry, that it was all but impossible to distinguish Hans from Kunz, so similar were they rendered by their environment. This and the quality of the entertainment conjures up Matthew Arnold's appalled confession in the 1860s, after warmly recommending German educational and political institutions, that he had never met a people as unattractive as the Germans.

There are many Germanies, of which this is only one. What would my own response have been if this had been the first image to hit me when I got off the train at Tübingen ten years ago? Or if, instead of the fountain in the lake of the town park, and the old houses scrambling up the Schlößberg from their own reflections in the Neckar, I had landed in the 'Bahnhofsviertel' of many a German town: the grey concrete, the endless motor traffic, the tatty snack bars and sex-shops? This image is changing: *Spießbürgertum* and its porky women (Neal Ascherson recollected how in the 1950s Germans would pride themselves on their wives: 'There, isn't she *fat!*') seems visibly dwindling away, even from the 'Rainbow-press' of the station bookstalls. But what is taking its place?

### Sarter's Folly

I

'The Drachenburg is open today' said the hand-written notice on the great wrought-iron gate. Beyond it, as in *Citizen Kane*, towers and minarets gloomed out of the evergreens. The green rack-and-pinion tram crawling past on its way to the Drachenfels on a cold, windy April day had few passengers and the Drachenburg, it seemed, no visitors at all. Inside the gate was a little hen-coop of a hut and a board from which the rain had washed most of the writing. I barely made out '17.00 Uhr' as the last guided tour, but as the hen-coop seemed inhabited – the windows were misted up – I tapped on its door. The window flew up and an elderly couple in identical red-and-white Scandinavian pullovers beamed out 'Selbstverständlich! Please go in.'

On the whole I dread guided tours, particularly German ones, but Peter Ehnes, by trade a carpenter, who has been administrator or, as he prefers, 'Castellan' of the Drachenburg for the last two years, since it was taken over by the North-Rhine Westphalian province, turned out an enthusiast for this weird building. It was as well that he did, because even after a lot of enquiry I can find little material on it, and this itself is significant.

Perched on the edge of the Siebengebirge, the Drachenburg is one of the most spectacular of the Rhine castles. But no-one is likely to imagine that it's old. It looks too much like a Victorian station hotel transplanted by a Wagnerian magician from, say, Middlesbrough. But its history is oddly emblematic of its time, and somehow of Germany itself. Paul Sarter, who built it, was born in 1820, the son of a local innkeeper, gone to the bad, who ended up making buttons in Cologne. Paul ran the financial side of the button business, was spotted by the Oppenheim brothers, and trained in their Paris and London banks. He forged useful alliances with them and the Rothschilds on one side, and Haussman and Ferdinand de Lesseps on the other. By the 1870s the Suez Canal and the rebuilding of Paris had made him a millionaire. He purchased a Barony and a 'von' from the King of Saxony, returned to his home town and bought up two-and-a-half square kilometres of the Siebengebirge above Königswinter. Obviously intending to make his mark, he commissioned the firm of Tüshaus and Abbema, Düsseldorf, to build his castle and acquired Hoffman, one of the architects who completed Cologne Cathedral, to do the Gothic detailing.

The dates of his project are almost identical with the building of Neuschwanstein in Bavaria by Ludwig II. Like Ludwig, von Sarter was besotted with Wagner, and he was almost as good on architectural siting, as the Drachenburg is practically at the point where, in 1867, the Master was inspired by the beauty of the Rhine Valley to write the prelude to the *Meistersinger*. Like Ludwig too, Sarter's castle felled him. He invested heavily in de Lesseps' Panama Canal project, lost, and had to pay back his creditors. The Drachenburg, which reputedly cost him forty million marks in the money of that day, was never lived in.

Von Sarter died, in relative poverty, in 1902. A nephew called Böttinger succeeded him, who let a select public in to view the murals of the *Nibelungenlied* by academic artists from Munich and the well-built girls who cavorted, less academically, across the ceiling of the *Bacchuszimmer*. This schoolboy's feast of bum and breast had to be covered up when the Brothers of Saint Michael moved in, after World War I. For the next two decades the place was a Catholic seminary, until the monks were evicted in 1939 by the Nazis, who used it as a Hitler Youth training school. They, and then the Americans, knocked it about a bit; most of the stained glass was shattered and a couple of towers picked off by artillery; and then, in the 1950s, it passed to another self-made man, a Herr

Spinat (spinach) who had also been born in poverty in Bonn and made a fortune in textiles during the *Wirtschaftswunder*.

Spinat set about restoring the Drachenburg on the cheap, with appalling results. A local artist with the talent of an eight-year-old 'restored' the damaged murals and left the Nibelungs looking like something out of Disney. When Spinat died, and the cracks caused by the wartime bombardment opened up, the *Land* government in Düsseldorf decided to pull it down. But local environmentalists protested, and the ministry changed its mind. When the money is forthcoming – and that may take time – the Drachenburg will become a museum of *Gründerzeit* (Victorian) architecture. Meanwhile Herr Ehnes remains Castellan, cropping the lawn ecologically with his flock of sheep, shooing them off the parterres and keeping the roof watertight.


II


'Restoration' in Germany is vigorous: on the neighbouring hill of the Petersberg, the hotel which served as the Federal guest house literally disappeared for a couple of years before reappearing in its Edwardian glory, rebuilt from the foundations up and plumbed with air-conditioning and security equipment for its privileged and not over-popular guests. Bristling with searchlights, armoured cars and soldiers with machine-guns, the Petersberg *is* the fortress the Drachenburg was only pretending to be.

There isn't in Germany that obsession with family and place so common in Britain. No National Trust persuades two-million odd to consider themselves part-owners of their heritage. There *can* be a fierce sense of local identity: the village or small town with its *Heimatmuseum*: sledges and yokes silvered with age, black-clad peasants squinting at the camera from the rutted fields of the 1890s. But in this fundamentally egalitarian society, the *Schlöß* was simply a bigger farmhouse, like the Rosenau near Coburg where Victoria's Albert was born. The great castle-builders, the Wittelsbachs or Hohenzollerns, slipping almost unnoticed out of German history in 1918, maintain only shadowy existences, even in the gossip columns. Volunteers are not going to give up weekends to stand guard in the state bedroom while the visitors pass round: hence the inevitable drone of the uniformed guide.

E M Forster wrote in *Howards End* that the Germans had the knack of getting, however crudely, to the heart of particular social situations, while the English, politely and atmospherically, waffled. The great houses of the *Gründerzeit* are the concrete expressions of the pretensions and the fears of the men who built them – something, intriguingly, more to be encountered in Wales or Scotland (think of Penrhyn Castle or Balmoral, which Albert designed). In the 1900s a sensitive cultural attaché at the German Embassy in London, Hermann Muthesius, discovered the subtleties of the smaller English country-house and recommended it to his countrymen as a frame for an unobtrusive sense of well-being and social solidarity. Scarcely a German town is without its suburb of Anglo-German villas, half timbered or harled, with details out of Rennie Mackintosh or Baillie Scott. World War I, as in Britain, brought this upper-class affluence to a precipitate end, but in Germany the country house, as a way of life, never really got started.

Even now, the Germans are wary of their architectural past. After twelve years of architectural fanaticism, in which anything with a flat roof was denounced as 'Jewish-cosmopolitan', the modern movement remains in possession: industrialists pose for interviews before uncomfortable abstracts in Le Corbusier style flats: machines for living in. The house and garden as culture-centre is something that happens in Tuscany, even in Britain, which still provides a spiritual home for many German intellectuals (a lawn is an 'English lawn'). There is a taste for the grand, in vast new museums of modern art where the rooms are usually more interesting than the paintings, but there isn't that mass of stately homes, or 'gardens open to the public in aid of the ambulance service' which strew 'heritage' across the country.

## III

Reading Walter Scott, Goethe remarked on the material richness of rural life he described, in contrast to the poverty of his own Hessian countryside. One can still see this in the 'Journeys through Art' which German television takes through Britain: the undisguised envy of the rambling mansion under its undulating roof, the squire in shirtsleeves at the village fete. The interesting thing is that this is not a mindless enthusiasm. The deformations of the 'heritage industry' are acknowledged; Patrick Wright, one of its sharpest critics, interviewed. The Germans seem to have cottoned on to another aspect of 'heritage': the fact that the house and the estate were social entities, and that there has been a struggle over their control, whose outcome – the sort of compromise reflected in the National Trust – represents the positive side of civil society in Britain, the richness that Joyce Cary invested in the country house of Tollbrook in *To Be a Pilgrim*: 'a wisdom and a faith so close to death and life that we could not tell what part of it was God's and what was man's sense; the sense of the common English, in a thousand generations'.

What Goethe complained of still exists, in terms of a narrowness of cultural possibility. The area around Stuttgart (roughly a million people) has only about a third of the mansions, museums, gardens in the area reachable from Glasgow. In the Mark of Brandenburg, around Berlin, which the novelist Theodore Fontane consciously used in his novels in the same way as his hero Scott had used Scotland, the Communists deliberately demolished 643 of the 779 castles and mansions which had survived the war, as Walter Ulbricht put it, 'to obliterate the last traces of Junkerdom from every village'. The Mark has now become the green lungs of Berlin, but all that this offers are hypermarkets, golf-courses and sub-Disneylands.

A year or so ago, after reading that the Japanese had built a replica Rothenburg ob den Tauber, and had shipped a Victorian baronial pile from Carluke and re-erected it, I suggested – not facetiously – that we should build *in* Scotland historical theme parks, which would double as Scottish cultural and trade centres, and then set these up in prosperous but particularly boring parts of Europe. Result, a lot of high-value-added employment at home and abroad, and an avoidance of the instabilities and uniformities of mass tourism. The more I think about the idea – which seems an apt combination of English subtlety and Scoto-Germanic force – the more I like it, not just because the role of Castellan, or Baron-Bailie, of the first of these joints could be taken, with great pleasure to himself, and relief to everyone else, by Sir Nicholas Fairbairn . . .

## II

Germany is a near-at-hand country about which the British, who have stationed an army there for nearly half a century, know surprisingly little. An army officer recently remarked on one reason for this: his men, monoglots who could nevertheless be guaranteed to 'pull a bird' within minutes of being set down in any German market-place, had now become 'video vegetables' fixated on violent or porno movies. Only one British politician – Denis Healey – has anything like a competent grasp of the language, and he is no longer in the front line. Getting Donald Dewar to view federalism 'live' in Bavaria proved a major operation, as he hadn't been out of Scotland for years and lacked a passport. For the rest, two assumptions – wildly contradictory – seem to apply. Because most German politicians speak impeccable English, affect Anglophilia, and are apologetic about the German past, a community of identity is assumed, which is not always the case. The second, latent in the swamps of the British popular press, hasn't changed in years. 'There are only two German stories: new Nazis and old Nazis'.

The British language deficit – 'Shout hard enough, and they'll understand!' – is serious, as it means that British coverage of German affairs is predominantly political (correspondents being based in Bonn, where nothing else goes on) and otherwise tends to conform to the old routines. German is essential to find out reactions to politics at local and *Land* level, and much British failure in technology and the applied sciences stems from the lack of it. English is the language of pure science, information technology and the service industries, but German is the language of technical innovation. Yet to understand it at some level of sophistication (not easy, it has taken me all of ten years) is to encounter a quality of pessimism and *Weltschmerz* in the politics of the language scarcely perceptible in the repertoire of the practised English speaker.

The ruins of the German cities have been rebuilt, sometimes crudely but often with great sensitivity, but the prestige of the language has never recovered from the damage inflicted – by the First rather than the Second World War. Carlyle, more than anyone else in Britain, was conscious of the German 'mission', and through Goethe, Schiller and Herder, Wagner, Marx and Nietzsche it influenced Coleridge, Thomas and Matthew Arnold, Shaw and D H Lawrence. World War I brought this hegemony to an end, with the displacement of German philology in English departments and the erection of Eng. Lit. into a system of national values. German as the great 'scientific language' was overthrown and, despite the contribution of post-Marxian philosophers in the inter-war period, was destroyed along with German Jewry. Where it irrupts today – where the British take an interest in what a German writer has to say – it tends to be purely as illustration to some political event.

The result is the half-regretful, half-defensive attitude of the Germans to a language which is cumbersome in some directions – particularly in the subtleties of politics, where *Politik* has to stand for half-a-dozen different English terms – and brilliantly lucid in others. *Umwelt* (world around) is a much simpler and effective word than environment, and any German child can master the Lego-like construction of more detailed terms and the simplicity of pronunciation. But the great and quite legitimate ambitions of the language ended in the horrors of the concentration camps, and the damage suffered then has left deep lesions in political and cultural life which re-unification didn't heal, and which the Gulf conflict has agonisingly reopened.

## Lava on the Grass: the German Right

### I

In the middle of the bombardment of Kuwait, as I was heading south to the Austrian lakes, I found a train toilet scrawled from top to bottom with political graffiti. 'US out of the Gulf' it said. 'No blood for oil' – which was what my students had been chanting a few days back – but then it went on: 'German troops out of Turkey: Turks out of Germany', 'Carve America into single states', 'No money for I\$rael', 'No immigrant state'. The German right was back, and seemed to have attached itself – as before – to some themes which seemed persuasive to left as well as right: fear of war and bombing, the legitimate detachment of a state which seemed to have made itself East Europe's sugardaddy from a conflict seemingly occasioned by the USA's spendthrift energy policies; the pressure exerted by a right-wing Israeli government whose own behaviour to its minorities was less than instructive.

My responses were influenced by two things: one was an essay by Enzensberger in *Der Spiegel* in which he had related Hitler's appeal to destruction and self-destruction to the *Demütigung* of a society: its abasement before problems it couldn't cope with, and the contempt of other societies. The other was a conversation that I'd had a couple of years before with Sir Frank Roberts, former British ambassador in Bonn, about Hitler. Roberts, as a student, had accompanied a Communist friend to a Nazi demonstration in Bonn around 1931 when unemployment had reached six millions, and Communists and Nazis had stretched the resilience of the Weimar republic to the limit. He said that he himself had been unimpressed by Hitler, but that his friend was almost exhausted by trying to defend himself against the man's almost hypnotic appeal.

This is not to suggest that the same thing would work in today's Germany. The *Rentner* swaying to and fro in a too-easily provided *Gemütlichkeit* may (according to most opinion polls) be more likely to share the views of the toilet politician, but they have experienced the consequences of *charisma* gone wild. Some of the young – generally the less well educated – show a more nationalist inclination than formerly, others are much more strongly internationalist. What is unreassuring is the lesson that can be drawn from *British* experience: the economic *Demütigung* of 1975-79 produced the appropriate charismatic leader in Mrs Thatcher. The Falklands War – in every other respect an absurd episode – won her an election and allowed her to accelerate that decline. The Gulf War, less absurd but from the point of view of national reconstruction, equally irrelevant, may help win the Conservatives a further spell in power.

In the course of this the English crowd as Orwell knew it, with 'its gentle, knobbly faces' seems to have departed, to be replaced (according to choice) by 'our boys' fighting their way round the world. Suppose the Gulf War and the collapse of Soviet Russia make the economic difficulties of the *Neuen Bundesländer* get worse instead of better; suppose the sugardaddy's protégés run out on him and the careful management of the state finances ends; suppose the European ideal shatters and Hans-Dietrich Genscher has no successor at the foreign ministry. Would there be cause for worry? 'Ernst und ehrlich', as German politicians are apt to say, I think there would. But the reasons for this are not straightforward, nor are they unique to Germany. In 1961 Richard Hughes wrote, in *The Fox in the Attic*

> ... suppose that in the name of emergent Reason the very we-they line itself within us had been deliberately so blurred and denied that the huge countervailing charges it once carried were themselves dissipated or suppressed? The normal penumbra of the self would then become a no-man's land: the whole self-conscious being has lost its footing ... In such a state the solipsist malgre-lui may well turn to mad remedies, to pathological dreaming; for his struggles to regain his footing would indeed be an upheaval from being's very roots ... gurgling up hot lava suddenly on to the green grass.

The menace of the right doesn't just assert itself when the customary usages of society are subverted by utopian expectation, and the almost inevitable disillusion that follows it; it can also root itself in the more immediate sense of social powerlessness that follows on more gradual social change.

## II

When I first moved to Germany, I had rooms in a tenement owned by a Herr M, high above the Old Town. M was a sad, gentle man, who appeared much older than he in fact was. He knew Scotland, but only as a prisoner in a desolate camp during the last war. He had hated the weather and had no desire to return. He was the son of a pharmacist who had been 'Doktor', and had come down in the social scale to maintaining business machines. Since these were now all based on microchip technology, he was not doing well. The corpses of old mechanical cash registers lay gathering dust in the corridors; drawers were packed with matchboxes and empty walnut-shells. 'Ich hab' eine Hamstermentalität', he would say. He collected books, too. Early editions of Grimm's tales, 'Max und Moritz' by Wilhelm Busch, dubious apologetics by Hans Grimm and von Papen. 'Ah, the problem with Hitler was that he was stupid. He did not know where to stop. We could have stood together against *die Russen* . . . ' Where would Herr M's sympathies have been in the 1930s? He was typical of the middle-class losers whom inflation, depression and the loss of status drove into an alignment with the Nazis. This group *is* dangerous, because it's intelligent enough, with its Speers and Goebbels, to market itself. And the *Mittelstand*, the small shopkeeper and craftsman sector which has been a reliable prop of centre-right politics, is steadily diminishing in contemporary Germany: in the 1980s alone from 48% to 27% of the retail trade.

National feelings, legitimate elsewhere, inevitably cause a *frisson* when expressed in German. The British media are beady-eyed when it comes to youths with flags. Nowhere in Europe is the far right harmless: Germany included. On the other hand its British inheritance – the drunken skinhead mouthing racialist abuse – makes it less appealing than the naive boy-scoutish *Parteijugend*, who vanished with the Free German Youth of the Honecker regime.The Republikaner and their leader Franz Schönhuber failed to surmount the 5% hurdle in the 1990 elections. Yet Germany, as much as Thatcher's England, is suffering the end of a traditional socialisation.

The half-timbered villages of Bavaria, surrounded by their open fields and orchards, have the same misleading antiquity as Sussex. But the elaborate metal inn signs may rear over Greek, Yugoslav or Italian restaurants, since *Gastarbeiter* occupy the older houses in the village centres. The gainers from the economic miracle are in the ranch-style or chalet-style estates on the fringe, with three-car garages and swimming pools; the losers drive 1970s Opels from decaying family farms or try to keep their little electrician's or tailoring business going, seeing themselves as threatened by the unions, by immigrants, by the Common Market, by the hypermarkets next to the motorway. For a highly-structured centre-right,

such privatisation of social life brings the problems the SPD politician Peter Glotz has identified in *The German Right*:

> The CDU and CSU as people's parties reach deep into an
> elaborate subculture about which the average liberal in our
> society now knows scarcely anything: hunting and shooting
> clubs, Leagues of Mary and the Adalbert Stifter societies. The
> crisis of the CDU/CSU stems from the feeling many conservatives
> now have, that these roots are dying . . . The right is no longer
> a menace to democracy, but has still the power to lock society
> into boring and torrid debates about the past.

Add to this fears about the environment, drugs and Aids, an
endemic housing shortage, the replacement of jobs by sophisticated
new technology, underdeveloped service industries which curb job-
creation for immigrants and the urban underclass (that effective
integrater the 'open all hours' corner shop is legally impossible
in Germany) – and a considerable residual racism – and one can
query Glotz's reassuring conclusion.


## III


Few attempts at interpretation were more inept than Mrs Thatcher's Chequers briefing on Germany. Starting from the premise of
a smooth process of unification, grand generalisations were made
about the German past and the German character. The fact was that
progress towards unity would *not* be smooth, because Germany
had stumbled into it through a sequence of events which were only
marginally to do with nationalism.

Before the collapse of the DDR, the right's major concern was to
recover from the death in 1988 of Franz-Josef Strauss, and prevent
the rise – as had happened in France – of a xenophobic far-right
party which might split the conservative vote. With Thatcher, there
was of course no need for such a party in Britain! Neal Ascherson
wrote that Strauss was 'one of these Germans who know what
democracy is, but not how to make it work'. His craving for
international recognition made him a 'model European'; his personal dynamism and the economic boom in south Germany made
him a 'bourgeois regionalist' who could also keep the Bavarian
right happy. Without him, nationalism of a cruder variety would
almost inevitably challenge the routine of the machine-men, who
have given the German constitutional right a hermetic quality closer
to Communist practice than to the looser politics of the SPD and
the Greens. Its leadership – Helmut Kohl is a typical example – is
recruited while at university and works its way up through the party

bureaucracy; its command of this makes it practically impregnable. But party institutions can be mortal.

Volker Ruhe, the General-Secretary of the CDU, recently bemoaned the fact that, if his boss Helmut Kohl had problems, no successor-generation was in sight. The well-doing have shifted away from politics, even physically away from Germany itself, into love affairs with Tuscany or that seemingly eternal German pilgrimage to exotic (but safe) holiday destinations. The disadvantaged, like Herr Munderkinger, seek the remaining *Stammtisch* or the archaic but well-heeled *Vertriebenen* groups representing refugees from Silesia, the Sudetenland and East Prussia. While the SPD has kept away from financial scandal for a decade, the Union's oligarchs have surprisingly primitive connections with big business, despite the latter's 'non-partisan' facade – Karl-Otto Pohl, late of the Bundesbank, and Edgar Reuter, boss of Daimler Benz are SPD members – and their involvement in scandals like the Flick affair has multiplied. The Union's building blocks – the Young Union, the women's and regional associations – remain well-organised bodies for ambitious right-wingers to cultivate, along with the *Vertriebenen* groups, but they are not conducive to civic virtue.

In 1988 the young minister-president of Schleswig-Holstein, Uwe Barschel, committed suicide. Barschel had risen in a *Land* CDU influenced by *Vertriebene* and ex-Nazis, and deployed a dirty tricks campaign in the 1988 elections against his SPD opponent Björn Engholm, and killed himself when found out. The result wasn't just a win for the SPD; it had longer-term implications. It dislodged Gerhard Stoltenberg, the regional CDU chief, and brought in as Bonn finance-minister the CSU's Theo Waigel, who proceeded to echo the *Vertriebenen* line, muttering darkly about restoring the frontiers of 1937. His party created an East German *Doppelgänger*, the DSU, and the CDU chased after it into the East German elections.

## IV

Fundamentally, only a minority of the West German population wanted full unity in 1990. How many West Germans, for example, have been to the east since the Wall fell? Among my students, friends and fellow-townsmen, not a lot. Genscher and Lambsdorff, both of them Liberals and Protestants, the latter truly the last of the Junkers, had real enthusiasm both for unity and for the free market; the Catholic CDU's support for both was strictly limited. But from late 1988 the structures of West German politics started to alter in ways which reflected the decay of the conservative political community, and in turn these reacted on political strategy.

The assault on the politics of East Germany was far more energetic than any observers had ever expected. The initial cries of 'Wir sind das Volk' (We are the people) became – with some assistance from the West – 'Wir sind *ein* Volk' (We are *one* people). Rapidly, the schemes adumbrated by Kohl himself, for a ten-year, ten-stage unification process; and the plan for an initially loose confederation between the two Germanies, with a distinct Eastern monetary system, exchanging at about two or three Ostmarks to the Deutschmark, collapsed. The way was open to a sharp and successful campaign in which the Easterners were persuaded to support Kohl, the CDU and the dubious affiliates of the 'Eastern' CDU as a sort of cargo-cult which would supply Western levels of prosperity simultaneously with the Deutschmark.

At one level this was a hands-down win for the Western political establishment. By the end of 1990 what had passed for a post-Honecker East German political class – Modrow, Böhme, de Maiziere – had virtually been wiped off the political screen. The highest-profile Eastern politician was Kurt Biedenkopf, Minister-President of Saxony and a former rival of Kohl in the Western CDU. But Biedenkopf was fairly unusual in involving himself in Eastern politics. The consultation processes of German society could not cope with the arrival of a large, poor relative on the national doorstep. The *Bundesrepublik* was as ill-equipped as the British had been when faced with Ireland and her problems in the early nineteenth century. Long-term planning looked like inflexibility, principle like naive obstinacy, business-government relationships alarmingly like corruption. Three episodes from recent German history seem appropriately disconcerting.

## Departures

### I

On Sunday 13 January 1991, as the Middle East countdown was noisily ticking towards zero, the Baden-Württemberg Minister-President, Lothar Späth, resigned. For some weeks stories had been appearing in the German press about over-intimate relations with industrialists; flights by Concorde to holiday islands, expensive yachts in the Aegean chartered for holidays and paid by German firms. Späth struggled: 'Späth is not to be bought; Späth is no playboy'. But he went.

Späth, always the *Cleverle* (little clever one), had timed his exit well, but it did a lot of damage to the structure of European inter-regional collaboration that he worked hard to set up. The suspicions increasingly voiced in Stuttgart that the premier was 'too often away on business' – started to ring true; the remarkable international impact made by this provincial German politician began to be put down to clever manoeuvring by big German firms – Grundig, Daimler-Benz, I.T.T. – who manipulated him and the local Christian Democrats in their own interest. The man who steered Baden-Württemberg for twelve-and-a-half-years (and was still only fifty-three) was substantially the originator of the European High-Technology Confederation to which Wales is affiliated. The question was now whether it could survive his departure. The *Staatsministerium*, Späth's self-created power-house (unique in German *Länder*), was purged as ruthlessly as Downing Street after She went. Would the high-profile foreign policy go with it?

Späth was a bit of a rascal, true, oddly similar to David Lloyd George: the low-class origins, the non-academic career, the ritual gestures of unity with the homeland, the wealthy and none-too-scrupulous friends. How much of the YMCA activist from Ilsfeld – about the size of Peebles – in the 1950s was there in the man who allowed Max Grundig to spend half a million Deutschmarks on his holidays? And yet, as with Lloyd George, qualities of vision and energy appear, which would seldom be encountered in Bonn – or London. Späth saw that, if regions were to stand up to the multinationals, they had to be equipped to do so. Hence his strategy of 'nationalising' technical innovation. He also realised that 'high tech' regions could get together to present the multinationals with a 'package'. They could make available co-ordinated facilities for research, development and training; this could also ensure that they were not undercut by poorer regions. His fall may have stemmed from trying to match these ambitions with the modest means available to anyone in German provincial government.

Wales came late into the Confederation, in March 1990, still only regarded as a second-class member. Yet it had a lot to offer: principally (and ironically) the English language. Among the 'Four Motors' it's obvious that collaboration remains laborious because of communication problems between four (or, if you count Spanish as well as Catalan, five) separate languages. The international language of new technology is English, and German students want to go to British universities because they're far more efficient. (A German MA takes about double the time of its British equivalent.) The one area where British institutions enjoy a potential lead is in the language and instructional field, but it presents mighty prospects of development, particularly in linking the 'Four Motors' with Eastern Europe.


## II


Almost as alarming had been the exit after the all-German elections of December 1990 of the Green party, which had attained its highest performance in Späth's *Land* of Baden-Württemberg. 'Everyone is talking about Germany. We talk about the weather.' The Greens' slogan was very witty in an English way, and serious in bringing up the subjects of smog, the ozone layer and global warming. But its vote slumped from 8.3 % to below the 5% line and it had to leave Bonn after seven years. The 'Ossies' – generally supposed to be more nationalistic and conservative – kept the Green flame burning (just) by returning eight MPs, but the defeat was a much greater setback than anything that can befall a British party, as expulsion from parliament meant the removal of state subsidy – around DM 12 million a year – and 90% of the party staff lost their jobs.

The party survived the *Land* elections in Hessen and formed a stable coalition ministry with the Social Democrats, so the German political future could still be red-green. So why the catastrophe? Its roots lie in the programme and organisation of the party, the sociology of its supporters, the response of the other parties, and the German political landscape in general.

The Greens are also known as 'Alternatives', indicating their link back to the 'Extra-Parliamentary Opposition' of 1968. The party founded in 1979 was an alliance between environmentalists and the 'revolutionary' left, between ecologists and libertarian Marxists. While the notorious split between *Realpolitiker* and *Fundamentalisten* did not exactly follow this division (some of the Marxists found it easier to get on with Social Democrats and industrialists than more 'committed' conservationists) this always produced tensions.

By their second term in Bonn, after 1987, it was obvious that *Realo* environmentalism appealed to the German business and union establishment – men such as Lothar Späth – who saw 'environmental engineering' as a means of industrial reconstruction. Business appreciated the research results coming out of Green think-tanks because they were pushing a consistent environmental, and not a party line; though this did little to reconcile the utopian socialists among the *Fundis*. In part these increasing tensions were mitigated by the impact of the peace and anti-nuclear campaigns, which missile modernisation and Chernobyl kept in the headlines throughout 1986. But as the cold war ended and the DDR broke up, it became apparent how criminally incompetent 'real existing socialism' had been in the environmental area, and unity became more and more difficult. The utopians either lapsed back into the sectarianism of the far left, or drifted away from politics into single issue groups or private life, while the *Realos* were hit both by the taking-over of their ideas by the SPD's Oskar Lafontaine's 'eco-socialism' campaign, and by the defection to the SPD of their highest-profile politician, Otto Schily.

Schily was always a marked man because *he wore a tie*. The Alternative scene is, in a Germanic way, as disciplined and ordered as the army, with jeans, sandals, long hair and pullovers the regulation uniform. Now you'll notice that all of this reeks of the radicalism of yesteryear, and the Greens fit pretty much into the 30–45 age bracket of the 'APO-Opas' (extra-parliamentary opposition grandfathers) as they are known to a harder and younger generation. Indeed most of them are to be found on the fringes of academic life, with the largest Green votes occurring in university towns like Freiburg and Tübingen. The problem is that this generation is small in proportion to German population as a whole, that the 'youth vote' is itself constrained by the fall in the birth-rate in the 1960s. Moreover, through a notably illiberal decision of the Federal Constitutional Court, the Greens can't involve sympathetic groups like *Gastarbeiter* in local politics.

In 1987 there were signs that the Greens were making inroads among the urban working class, at the expense of the SPD, but their subsequent decline has partly been the result of ideological burglary by the other parties. Energy conservation and the taxation of polluting activities have become major planks of government policy, and environmental goals are now taken into account in the annual assessment of the German economy. Throwaway bottles, artificial fertilisers, phosphates in washing powder, unnecessary packing material, the car itself, have been cast more and more into question. The cause of feminism was also given a remarkable boost, in a country in which the old circumscriptions of 'Kinder, Küche, Kirche' died hard. In 1983, a woman's ultimate possibility in politics would be the 'family and social welfare' portfolio; now there are 40% female cabinets in most SPD *Länder*, and the most popular politician after Hans-Dietrich Genscher is the liberal-minded Christian Democrat academic Rita Süssmuth. With a 'cleaner' SPD since the days of the Flick party finance scandal, which Schily helped expose, one Green interpretation sees 'consolidation' as hopeless: the party can only maintain its distinctiveness by being more radical. Ex-*Realo* refugees like Schily have seemed to confirm this by getting out. The Greens were aided by seven years of Kohl's centre-right bumbling in Bonn, which caused a leftward shift in the *Länder* and *Communes*, while Bonn intervened less at this level. German politics have become more regional, with Red-Green alliances quite frequent at local level, and new political agendas. On the other hand regionalism made it difficult for the left to handle the unexpected issue of German unity and the appearance on the scene of 15 million people whose main objection to Western consumerism was that they hadn't had enough of it. The economic stagnation and environmental mess in the DDR became simultaneously a stick to beat socialism with, and an excuse for lapsing back into the 'mindless growth' of the *Wirtschaftswunder* years, something which could yet reject the transplant of green policies into the German body politic.

The Greens tied into German parliamentary politics people who were intensely suspicious of them: a safety-valve which prevented the radical excesses of the 1970s, and fed new ideas into the political system. But this transferred the parliamentary/anti-parliamentary stand-off *into* in the party, and ultimately tore it apart. Even if *Realos* like Joschka Fischer and Antje Vollmer manage to reconstruct the party, a lot of frustrated direct-actionists on the left may drift away from constitutional politics – with unemployment in the East and a revival of left- and right-wing street-fighting politics providing a disturbingly large stack of combustible material.

## III

For election campaigns the Bundesbahn lays on special trains for the parties. These are, rather creepily, made up of the stock used by the leading Nazis to tour round the country during the years 1933–45, and are loaded with office equipment and free meat and drink for the accompanying journos. My friend David Gow was travelling around on the SPD's special in November 1990 and reported that the 'barracks' end of the train (the barracks is the modern-movement SPD headquarters in Bonn) was not communicating with the candidate and the 'fear and loathing' count would have been good going for the pre-Kinnock 'come on in the blood's lovely' Labour party conferences.

The SPD was duly slaughtered. Something had gone adrift in the SPD's matching of man and time. Lafontaine was the urbane man of German post-industrial society: high-tech 'flexible specialisation', European regionalism, art galleries, town planning schemes, dry white French wine, good-looking blondes who run art galleries and drink dry white French wine, whereas Kohl seemed like one of these huge statues that Germans in the Wilhelmine period plonked on top of any hill they could lay their hands on: solid, boring, but *there* and reliable.

Lafontaine embodied Enzensberger's 'Italianisation of Europe', but his regional sophistication was the product of Kohl's abstention from interference in *Land* politics. Lafontaine only differed in degree from him, or from Späth in Baden-Württemberg, in his links with German finance and industry, and support for tax regimes to promote industrial restructuring according to environmental priorities – public transport, detoxification of land and water. His scheme for an incomes and employment policy – restaining wages order to create jobs – was more positively accepted by business than by the unions.

Yet by cultivating prosperous Wessis worried about being 'swamped' by incomers from the East and asylum-seekers, he strengthened the impression in the East that the SPD 'doesn't want us', *and* emphasised the appalling legacy of 'forty years of real existing socialism'. The impression he gave, as prime minister of the country's smallest province, not much bigger than Lothian Region, and someone who scarcely bothered to campaign in the east – was a 'Kleinburger' only concerned with the size of the bill, while Kohl was the big man prepared to take on big responsibilities – 80 million of them.

This solidity proved illusory. Within a couple of months the SPD was taking more CDU-run *Länder*, including Kohl's own state, which his party had run for over forty years. But, worryingly, turnouts at the elections steadily fell to British levels. After a period when politics was something redemptive, which the Germans worked very hard at, they seemed to have lapsed into cynicism. This seemed particularly true of the SPD, traditionally the more European of the German parties. A very able generation had come up in the party, winning *Land* elections and setting up interesting, experimental, regimes, yet at a European level the suspicion of being *kleinkariert*, tuppeny-ha'penny, Mickey Mouse politicians hung around them. When Lafontaine visited Washington he was received by Bush with more dignity than Reagan had shown Neil Kinnock, but made an even worse impression – 'like a little provincial mayor complaining about the bill for lunch' according to an SPD friend.

Party centralisation has usually been held against proportional representation, and it played a part here. In all continental parties, there are too many who fit into an administrative-academic frame

and not enough representing housewives or *Gastarbeiter*, pensioners or unemployed school leavers – or capable of giving them the
sense that they are part of the political community. Oratory,
crowds, emotion had got Germany into bad trouble before, but
the absence of an emotional content – of Benns and Healeys and
Sillarses – could almost be as bad in lowering the attraction of the
democratic system. The Friedrich Ebert Stiftung does much more
work in Britain for the Labour party than any British socialist body
does in Germany, but collectively, the various European socialist
parties are still as far away from creating a socialist imagination for
Europe as they were in 1980. As the key to taming multi-national
capital is a strong left in a more powerful European parliament,
this gap is more than worrying.

## From Blut und Boden to Country and Western

### I

Over less than a year, the image of Germany in the British press
changed from proto-superpower, ready to launch itself, as of old,
on to the European scene, to that of a war-shy 'political dwarf'.
Norman Stone contrived to hold both positions, doing his bit at the
Chequers briefing and beating a drum for the allies in the *Sunday
Times*. Germany didn't share the West's enthusiasm for large-scale
war. But a foreign service focussed under Hans-Dietrich Genscher
on Eastern Europe and an internal pluralism meant that Bonn lost
track of what exporters in the *Länder* were up to. Disastrously.
What sort of system of political interpretation allowed a powerful
and well-informed country to make such mistakes, and end up
being dragged by the United States and Britain, its two biggest
debtors, into paying for a war it couldn't control in a region where
it had (in comparison to Eastern Europe) few essential interests?

Even more alarming, this *Ohnmacht* coincided with the collapse
of what remained of the East German economy. Its adaptation
to capitalism, as one ex-Communist put it, resembled a non-
swimmer tossed overboard in a storm. By early 1991 not only
heavy industries and agriculture faced going under, but the local
and *Land* authorities, whose taxation base dwindled as unemployment rose. From being a European opportunity, East Germany
rapidly turned into a German disaster. The magnitude of the
undertaking – organising and motivating people drawing less than
half the Western level of wages and salaries – proved beyond the
West German political culture.

## II

The classic example of this culture at its best and worst is the German Federal Railway. Its timetable is legendary. It is huge, weighing nearly 4 lbs. It is helpful, providing a footnote for every possible eventuality (the 8.47 from Bampotstein to Markt Hummdinger carries suitcases, but bicycles only on Saturdays which are also schooldays); and it requires a Ph.D to make any sense of it. The June 1991 issue was remarkable by any standards, being valid for a whole year, featuring the *Bundesbahn* and the old East German *Reichsbahn*, and the 'Inter-City Expresses' which at £18 million a go, were to shrink the time of a Hamburg-Munich journey from nine and a half to seven and a half hours.

But where and what is Bad Zwischenahn? This obscure spa somehow got itself on to the cover, pushing Berlin to the back and evicting the Inter-City Express completely: a coup for the Herr Kurdirektor, but a horrendous reminder that – for all its technical brilliance, its courteous staff and its reasonable fares – a business the *Bundesbahn* is not. It is a branch of the civil service, its marketing skills are on that level, and its deficit has reached a stupendous 15 billion Deutschmarks, even before it falls heir to the clapped-out equipment of the Reichsbahn. It is not just on the railways but in the universities, where the ebbing of the 'spirit of '68' has left an inflexible and inefficient professorial hierarchy, in the broadcast media, economic and agricultural pressure groups, where the weaknesses of Germany most show up. In all of these the burden of the past has yet to be dissolved by more informal and liberal structures.

In the universities a professorial hierarchy is important in the natural sciences, where millions have to be raised from grant-awarding bodies and industrial firms; but the senior academic will also be aware that his clout comes from the skill and initiative of his younger colleagues. In the humanities the fact that the German structure of professorial recruitment is quite separate from the lecturer grade perpetuates a situation where a chair can be regarded as a terminus rather than a jumping-off point. While research and teaching have the resources to be much more co-operative and imaginative, many younger academics leave the system in frustration, and there is no career structure at all for the majority of humanities graduates: women. This effectively isolates much of the intelligentsia from effective intervention in political life. 'The University of Tübingen is to the University of Oxford', John Ardagh wrote in the mid-1980s, 'what British Leyland is to Daimler-Benz'. I have my local patriotism, but I take his point.

In television the number of channels has mightily increased, because of satellites, received via the state programme which has plumbed the country with fibre-optic cable. But the linking jingles, the adverts, the continuity, haven't changed since Adenauer's day. German television, like the railways, definitely falls into the 'social' part of the 'social market' economy. It is there as a public service, for prestige, as a monument to German engineering, and only secondarily as a form of competitive entertainment. There are two ways of regarding the TV challenge. The box *qua* window on the street of the global village and the box *qua Zuschauer-Schnuller* (viewer's dummy) can be compatible. Switching public service TV on for an evening is still to invite a surprise, when they take 'Problems of our time No.7: Acne' off the prime time slot and run a special report on the Arab-in-the-Amman-Street's reaction to the bombing of Baghdad. But this element will diminish as the choice of channels increases: the familiar and emollient will come easier to hand.

Again, the *Bundesbahn* effect. Take the German version of *Spitting Image. Hurrah Deutschland!* was promoted like a new airliner; hordes of technicians spent millions and worked for months on the puppets. And, right, they looked alive. You felt for them as they waded through a rotten script. No-one seemed to have considered that *Vorsprung durch Technik* by itself wasn't exactly a bundle of laughs.

German TV is still quite impressive in a Reithian way. Its documentaries are very subtle and sensitive, as are its current affairs, health, science and environment programmes. In political cabaret (for those streetwise enough to catch the allusions) and above all in the arts, Germany is the last redoubt of the old radical *avant-garde*. A little of Joseph Beuys goes a long way; but in Germany arts coverage seems to express enthusiasms, and not to dramatise press releases. But German television isn't a distinct experience: it's a collection of programmes, lacking informality, a magazine format, viewer involvement, and hence absurdly vulnerable to the slick emptiness of the satellite channels.

The explanation for this backwardness shows the burden of history. In the 1920s and early 1930s, aided by the Leica camera, the Germans pioneered photo-journalism. Many of the magazines that then appeared were radical and often Jewish-run, and exiles from them helped set up the British photo-journals *Picture Post* and *Illustrated* in the 1930s. As these couldn't carry programme details, unlike their German counterparts, they faded out under the assault of TV in the 1950s. But their magazine style shifted over to TV, as the BBC reacted to competition from the new commercial channels. Many of the personalities of *Tonight*, he first of the magazine programmes, were graduates of *Picture Post*, and so too was the general format – something which in due course disseminated itself over the whole evening's viewing.

In David Hare's TV play about wartime black propaganda, *Licking Hitler*, two Jewish refugees are brought to the radio studio to broadcast in the character of disillusioned German officers. Their first attempt is dreadful. One looks at the other and shrugs despairingly, 'I thought we Jews were supposed to be good at showbiz.' There were, of course, precious few such showbiz adepts around in Germany after 1945, and the continuing absence of a Jewish population has taken its toll of the state's imagination. In a peasant-dominated, localised country the ravages of marauding armies made it prudent to keep one's head down and shut up. 'Mein Name ist Hase, und ich weiß von nichts' (I'm only a hare and don't know anything about anything) hasn't, significantly, got an English equivalent. The Jews were urban, intellectual, vocal. They were in place to take advantage – as entrepreneurs, bankers, publicists – of an industrialisation which was rapid, insensitive and unbalanced, and carried out under a sequence of deeply reactionary governments. They benefitted from this and rationalised the process, yet as a confession they stood aside from the state system, which lacked the British tradition's openness to the culture of self-governing sects. They tried to embrace that system, with a more thorough-going enthusiasm than they showed in England – 'Wilhelmine Culture' in its strengths and weaknesses is in great measure a Germanic-Jewish culture – but that system turned on them, menaced them, and then when it collapsed, destroyed them. The *Bundesrepublik* benefitted enormously from a flood of German immigrants from the conquered East, but it has never compensated for this haemorrhage of adaptive talent.

## III

'Yes, I think we've *experienced* Reit am Winkl. Now let's get out.' I overheard an Englishman in Bavaria, and whatever my own loyalties, I knew exactly what he meant, and agreed. This 'picturesque' Bavarian village was hell on earth, or at least four wheels: totally similar to twenty or so other villages in the neighbourhood but particularly crowded because it figured – rather like Memphis, Tennessee – as a centre for the 'Volkstümlichen Melodien' relayed by television. Reit seemed to embody the wealth of West Germany, the worst aspects of its lack of imagination, and in the 'Volkstümlichen

Melodien' – properly considered, a German version of Country and Western – the flight from a history whose reality had to be confronted.

The weakness of television, tourism and entertainment reflects a West Germany deeply and defensively impregnated by legal structures which not only throttle the development of a lively, informal civil society but also destroy much of what they're supposed to preserve. Shop-opening legislation rules out the integration of immigrant groups in a more flexible service sector, particularly important in the East. Leisure facilities are well-financed but unimaginatively-organised and the general overstressing of individual acquisitiveness suggests that an extended check on prosperity might provoke unpleasant reactions. Part of this uncertainty stems from a *Land* identity which remains essentially political and economic rather than social and cultural, even after forty years. Yet the old 'particularism' might, if given its head, exacerbate some of these problems. In 1928 Lion Feuchtwanger wrote *Success*, in which the rough but sentimental Bavarians revered Ludwig II, carried out appalling perversions of justice, and harboured Adolf Hitler. The same Bavarians still deny the local vote to other EC nationals who may have worked there for decades. Oskar Lafontaine argued in the 1990 election campaign for a *Land* identity which would be cosmopolitan as well as regional, but his humiliating defeat showed that this will require a considerable change in German public opinion, not just on the right.

Leaving aside the problems of adapting the economy of the former DDR, Germany remains in many ways tentative, uncertain and bureaucratically inflexible, still subject (quite properly) to a sense of war-guilt, and despite its hegemonic position, distrustful of that sense of German 'mission' that powered both Bismarck and Marx. United by shrewd diplomacy and the collapse of a grotesque Stalinist necrocracy, the 'triumphalism of the West' has still to overcome a crude materialism and an unimaginative legalism which could dissolve the idealistic element in the German tradition, as drastically as World War II ended the authoritarian tradition.

## IV

The West German *Länder* have proved the practical prototype of a federalised and regionalised Europe. When the Treaty of Rome was signed in 1957 the *Bundesrepublik* was the only federal state within it. Now, apart from the smaller members, all states have introduced some form of semi-federalism, and Belgium has now adopted a formal federal constitution in order to resolve its linguistic divisions. Britain remains unique in resisting decentralisation – a course which has in no way been confirmed by any economic success. Germany has, on the other hand, gone beyond internal federalism in establishing a system whereby *Länder* can supervise EC activities, either individually through their own EC ministers and representation in Brussels, or collectively through the second chamber of the federal parliament, the *Bundesrat*, which now spends about half its time on EC legislation. (Until the next European parliament elections, the *Neuen Bundesländer* have only observer status at Strasbourg.)

The project of regionalism throughout Europe – earlier linked with the problems of agricultural districts – has obviously revived itself on the back of this federal success. In all this, the German example is ambiguous. The German structure has proved that it can deal very sensitively with mounting transport, demographic and ecological problems, which have assumed a priority inconceivable in the United Kingdom. This has been in part a response to a technical challenge, in part the exploitation of an economic opportunity, in part perhaps a restitution of the past, a desire to prove that the Germans can redeem themselves.

At the same time *Land*-consciousness can be restrictive, with the horizons of the political and intellectual elite scarcely reaching across the *Land* boundary: something ominously evident in attitudes to the East. The rest of Europe has to recognise this ambiguity: the combination of seriousness, diffidence and guilt that marks the German approach to issues that its people, rightly, perceive as critical. And yet, also the sense that Germany's inclination, as well as right, to preach and to warn, has evaporated.

## By Tram to Outer Mongolia

### I

The postcards I sent from Erfurt arrived with friends and relatives after spending two months travelling from the former German Democratic Republic to Britain, ninety per cent of the time being taken to cover the fifty miles to the former frontier at Bebra. We crossed that frontier in the November twilight, the 'express' clanking over the Thuringian hills at about twenty-five miles an hour. To the south, on the skyline, was a huge, glittering white mountain of mineral waste, unexplained and rather sinister. An hour later and the Erfurter Hof, our destination, loomed up opposite the main railway station.

The station square was all but silent, but then a metallic whining, once familiar in the canyons of central Glasgow, made itself heard. A tram appeared, a Number Three, destination Ulan Bator. It clanged through narrow, twisting medieval streets to the Domplatz, its cobbled expanse dominated by the stunning grouping of the thirteenth-century Cathedral of the Blessed Virgin and Saint Severin's Church. Unbombed, riding out the systematic neglect of an atheistic regime, was the great medieval city where Luther studied.

The Erfurter Hof had been a watering-hole for the *Parteibonzen*. Here in 1971 Willy Brandt and Willy Stoph, the East German president, put the seal on *Ostpolitik*. Vast wood-panelled rooms with deep armchairs, stained-glass screens from the glass-works at Lauschau not far from the totalitarian grandeur of the Carlton, the Nazi equivalent in Nuremberg: but with the DDR's temperamental plumbing. Mussolini made the trains run on time, and Hitler made the toilets flush. Real existing socialist plastic had to cope with the gargantuan breakfasts prepared for Wessi businessmen.

If you wanted to drive yourself mad you could count Trabbis – like counting pigeons in Trafalgar Square. But not for long; the little whizzing two-strokers were giving way to second-hand Wessi cars. Rumour had it that some newly-evolved microbe would be used to eat their plastic-and-papier maché bodies. In the pedestrianised main street, the Anger, rich in the civic architecture, from baroque to *Jugendstil*, which was usually pulverised in West Germany by bombing and post-war 'reconstruction', scaffolding was up around some of the thirty-two medieval churches: restoration with the help of the Rhineland city of Mainz, whose Archbishop ruled Erfurt until 1802. The fine medieval collection of the Anger Museum was being evicted to make way for the Thuringian *Landtag*.

Taking the Number Three tram to its destination the next day provided quite a different experience. Who else but German Communists would have christened a system-built housing estate 'Outer Mongolia'? Its grim four-storey blocks marched over the surrounding hills, all too redolent of Glasgow's Castlemilk – although with the difference (in Erfurt's favour) that the town centre was only ten minutes and fifty *Pfennig* away by tram. The new order had already captured the slab of a Culture Centre: a male-and-female striptease festival . . .

'Little Venice' was discouraging. The 'Merchant's Bridge' over the river Werra in the centre of the old town, with timbered houses on both sides, has been restored, but the northern part of the old town was either left to rot – or, worse, crushed underneath Mongolian monsters which had slouched in from the suburbs. From the crumbling Petersberg fortress above the Cathedral, the townscape by the station was dominated by the concrete hulk of a 'palace of culture', half-built and never likely to see an opening day.

## II

Erfurt university was abolished by its new Prussian rulers in 1816, but the Thuringian Land government is now trying to promote Erfurt as the site for a new European university. Such an initiative is badly needed. A few weeks later I was on a Bonn committee interviewing six shy girls from the old DDR. For the last couple of years I have been a member of the German Academic Exchange Service which selects candidates for scholarships at British universities. Not a huge success of academic co-operation as British university fees have made holes in the DAAD budget and the number of students supported has halved since 1980 to 60. Still, with last year's events in mind, the Bonn government increased the number of scholarships to 75, reflecting the increase in the Federal Republic's population. Given 300 applicants there ought to have been 60 more from the New Federal Lands.

There were twelve, all well below the level of 'Western' candidates. Why? Publicity was bad. The eastern universities were in an administrative mess, incapable of giving of detailed and patient academic advice. But structural problems within the existing East German system made it difficult for them to compete, even when all things were equal intellectually. Their vocabulary confirmed Orwell's fears in *1984*, a book that most had at last managed to read. And *Didaktik* had left its mark:

'What British authors have you read?'

'Charles Dickens.'

'Which of his books?'

'*Hard Times*.'

Ask a stupid question . . . But none of them had read *Hard Times* in English. They had read a German translation, along with extracts from the original English. Ideology and hierarchy had dominated the system – and continued to do so. All my colleagues had their horror stories. Attempts at collaboration frustrated by Eastern colleagues shy of responsibility. Cheques to fund book purchases which were never cashed; donated equipment which still had to be picked up.

'It will take at least two or three years until we have movement over there.'
'You must be joking. A generation.'

## III

In West Germany, academic life isn't adapted to innovation or rapid decision-making. Its attempts at speedy intervention in the Eastern universities, led by ministry officials from Bonn and their *alten Füchsen* (old foxes) advisers, ended in insensitive purges. Pluralist babies were thrown out with the Stalinist bathwater. As for missionaries *in partibus infidelium*, a recent survey which showed that only 2% of *Wessis* would go East for a holiday, let alone work there. Neglect breeds resistance. On our last night in Erfurt the station square filled up with football fans: inarticulately mutinous, like young bullocks, they banged up against bewildered and tactless policemen. Would they become the Ossi equivalent of 'our boys', customers for the twaddle and prejudice of Rupert Murdoch's *Super*? Or something a lot worse?

This huge educational problem gives a chance for Britain and Scotland. English was second to Russian in the GDR's schools and universities, but is the key to high technology and business studies. Initiatives from the British Council have already won praise, but a more ambitious project would put British educational institutions in a good marketing position, with their expertise in distance education. West German *Länder* and universities could use British distance-learning techniques and materials to supply their 'twins' in the East, bridging the period until new academic cadres are ready. But after 1992 academic qualifications will be interchangeable within the EC. Bright West German students in subjects like law and economics may want to opt for a short if expensive course at a 'British University in Germany' rather than putting in seven or eight years in the German system.

Why not team up with some *Länder* – east and west – and turn over the higher education budget of the British Army of the Rhine (soon to be withdrawn) to help set this up? It would, of course, only offer a limited range of courses – economics, business studies and the social sciences, history with the accent on postwar Europe, law, languages, education – but it could transmit these by Open University-type means, and operate on the Robin Hood principle of charging market rates to young Wessis who want to take their degree rapidly, and making available plentiful bursaries to the East.

In Erfurt? Perhaps. It's difficult to leave the dark, Kaspar David Friedrich-like woods of the Thuringian hills, in which the last of the tiny German principalities held out until 1918, so compelling is the atmosphere of that 'good' Germany to which the British romantics looked. At Weimar, only twenty minutes away from Erfurt by train, are the palaces of the little court of Saxe-Weimar-Eisenach, the church where Bach was organist, Schiller's house. Goethe's dwelling-house, on the Frauenplan seems, despite the mass of tourists, and the large museum devoted to the poet, playwright, scientist and statesman, father-figure to the young Carlyle, still of the 1830s. The little garden, bitten by the frost but with its labelled plants, the summer-house with its geological specimens, await the return of its owner. In 1832 in a small room off his study, where he had corresponded with Walter Scott – then sailing, a mortally sick man, down the Rhine – he called for 'more light!' and died.

## *The Watch on the Rhine*

### I

In Germany in August I switched the television on and saw another boy in a silly lurid T shirt, laughing at the camera the way all kids do. Behind him stretched a street which could be anywhere here-abouts: wide-eaved houses, Coca-Cola signs, parked cars. Some of the cars were smouldering and a column of smoke rose in the distance. The kid disappeared as the camera swung rather agitatedly rightwards. Beside one car lay a metal coffin, its lid some distance away, as if both had been flung down from a hurrying lorry. On the other side of the car two feet protruded at an awkward angle. A series of snapping noises, and the camera cut to the column of smoke, roofs, and then down to the face of one of German television's young reporters, crouching behind a wall and very scared.

I have never visited Yugoslavia, though I've travelled in Carinthia, which has a Slovene minority, and seen where at Rosendorf the Vienna-Lublijana railway tunnels through the Karawanken mountains. Now the drab green carriages of the Yugoslavian railways were lying in sidings at Munich, refugees were trickling across the frontier, and the Austrians and Germans were getting very nervy. Last time I had stayed in a small inn above the Attersee, in a tourist area badly hit by the collapse of the American trade following the Gulf emergency. The landlady morosely watched the big television screen in the bar, and brightened a bit when the face of Jorg Haider of the FPÖ came into shot. 'That is a good man.' Haider, a pan-Germanist with a strong anti-Slav line, was thrown out as Governor of Carinthia in mid-1991 when he went too far in endorsing the Nazi past. By September his party was getting 15% in the Styrian provincial elections. Echoes of a disturbing past were returning.

Germany had achieved its unity. It had been managed with a lot of cleverness but its effects had plunged the country into a lengthy, painful political crisis which reflected little credit on the Conservative-Liberal government. In the same week as the film of civil war in Yugoslavia was coming through, the Christian Democrats were locked in a dispute with their Eastern wing, trying to purge it of the ex-Communist *apparatchiks* they had been eager to take on board – with their money, equipment and offices as a tocher – in 1990. Less than inspiring.

## II

The paradox of liberalisation was that it delivered power to politicians, people whom, in the Western democracies, no-one much approved of. Crowds were positive. They or their placards were saying (often, helpfully, in English) 'Down with Ceausescu/Honecker/Jaruzelski!' or 'We are the People!'. They shook their fists in photogenic squares. Those in whom they invested their support were visually disappointing. Without children or banners they sat in their horseshoe seats, impassive, like students at a particularly boring lecture. 'Men – and women – in suits' who seemed to bear out Robert Michels' old line: 'Two MPs of different parties have more in common than two members of the same party, one of whom is an MP'.

The same feeling had pervaded the later stages of the 1848 revolutions. The parliaments rapidly lost the people's attention – once they had got what they wanted: notably rights to their land. German *literati* and civil servants argued themselves into the ground at Frankfurt, discussing the shape of a putative liberal Germany: the peasantry took the land and let the troops of Prussian King and Austrian Emperor drive the talkers forth. 'Blood and Iron' in an odd way appealed more than democracy because service in the forces was something collective, the only significant new experience for the male population of a largely rural society which remained unpoliticised until the Nazi period. The urban minority were left with socialism and the institutions of the trade union movement, professional sport, and various somewhat toxic competitors: 'patriotism' variously defined, anti-semitism, imperialism.

Most of these options were suddenly closed off in 1991: militarism by the end of confrontation, collectivism by the 'end of socialism'. Agricultural failure was a root cause of the breakdown of the command economies, but over most of northern Europe there was no longer a significant rural population and the 'farming interest' was about as popular as the former Central Committees. This left constitutional politics and the market: the mixture which conservatives like Joseph Schumpeter, in *Capitalism, Socialism and Democracy* (1942) had seen as peculiarly unstable.

My mind went back to a conversation I'd had nearly twenty years before with John O'Sullivan, then married to a colleague at the Open University and a leader-writer on the *Daily Telegraph*, later a speech-writer to Mrs Thatcher. Commenting on the recent overthrow of Allende's 'popular front' regime in Chile, O'Sullivan argued that an authoritarian regime might be necessary to introduce a functioning market economy. Arguments of a cognate sort surfaced in that moment when in August 1991 the old guard briefly seemed to have taken over in Russia; a *Times* commentator assured us that Russian conservatives had been looking at authoritarian patterns of transition to markets, in Chile, China and Korea. The implication was that, however regrettable the suppression of democracy might be, stability and predictability, the reassuring elements of the Cold War, could be counted on. Even now, I suspect, this inclination remains: the Marxist-Leninist management buyout team has fumbled its chance, but offers are still open.

By the end of 1991 it was dawning on politicians that, as the waters of Communism receded, an older political geography was being uncovered. The collapse of Russia offered plenty of scope for great power manoeuvre: the prospect of a German sphere of influence extending to the Urals, of Japanese domination of Siberia and China. If the USA remained for the moment the one Superpower, its own economic problems constrained any possibility of its becoming world policeman. Hence the CIA's forecast of a future American-Japanese conflict. Primitive though his economics were, Orwell's Oceania-Eurasia-Eastasia seemed to be taking shape, or rather, geo-politics were reverting to the situation at which his 'authorities' – J A Hobson, Albrecht Haushofer, Halford Mackinder – saw the world in 1914. World population may have trebled since then, but the Kuwait crisis showed that the 'heartland', that tract between the Balkans, the Gulf and central Asia – now also the worlds's major non-nuclear energy source – remains as attractive to conventional nationalist politicians, Arab and non-Arab, as honey to bears.

Outside the Gulf, this last week in September, Belgian and French troops invade Zaire, Britain maintains its Falklands garrison, Germany seeks a peacekeeping force in Croatia. There is an odd similarity with the manoeuvres of second-rate politicians in the 1890s – Caprivi, Rosebery, Jules Ferry, Crispi – scrambling for Empire and natural resources, limply supervised by conservative parliaments of declining prestige. But, compared with a century ago, the environment our nation-states venture into, like elderly tourists, is so much more dangerous.

Back home, in Fife country towns or the valleys of the Black Forest, even regional or local politicians are now faced with problems terrifying enough in themselves. AIDS, drugs, intensive agriculture and over-motorisation, with their impacts on climate and health, are only some of the threats now facing us. Beyond them lie the greenhouse effect and global warming, the depletion of the rain-forests and ozone layer, overpopulation and desertification, any of which, singly, could have the same lethal effect. A new *Volkerwanderung*, a tidal wave of East European poor, might sweep down on the prosperous West. And what would happen if any of these problems were to be combined with one another – if environmental threat became aggravated by political instability – as with the burning of the Kuwaiti oil wells? If there had been a civil war in Russia in August 1991, what of the numerous potential Chernobyls? The former dissident Lev Kopelev asked *that* question in a *Die Zeit* interview in September. He did not even mention the nuclear weapon stockpiles . . .

## III

Here I am, walking along a leafy lane in Bad Godesberg, Germany, thinking about spring, birdsong and the like, when a limo swerves across and jerks to a standstill at my feet. And who do I see but my old friend Douglas Jones, who is padding around Europe on my spoor, from Edinburgh to Stuttgart and now back to Bonn, where he is caretaking for Ambassador Walters while Walters gets to play golf with the President in Kennebunkport. Which is big stuff for Doug, the American Embassy being as big as most German ministries even if it looks like a sanatorium, while the Consulate in Edinburgh is small and thin. I am remembering that Douglas thinks that interesting things are going on in Scotland which don't figure in what he's told by Malcolm Rifkind and similar dudes, and consequently regret his translation to the Rhineside dorf, and the vicinity of Hans-Dietrich Genscher, known to the trade as Genschmann, who is now around for five years longer than the late Hitler and better liked.

Bonn is the sort of place where Runyon-like rackets seem to be endemic. The embassies and legations throng the quiet streets of Bad Godesberg, as if every bungalow in Davidson's Mains had been taken over by Zaire or Cameroon or Singapore, the Mercedes parked in the driveway, the ambassadorial kids being shepherded off by the maid to the international school. I walk along the pavement, under the violent pink of the flowering cherries, and think about GNP per capita: $14,500-plus for the house on the corner (the Netherlands – scarcely fifty miles away: do they even *need* an embassy here?), $1,240 for Colombia (bet *he*'s glad to be away from home), $160 for Guinea-Bissau. None of them particularly grand, and none of their inhabitants up to the sort of naughtiness that seems to appeal in London. The *dolce vita* of Bonn lives down to W C Fields' great line: 'I went to Philadelphia, but it was closed'. But they are all here to play the diplomatic fruit machine, some on behalf of their countries, some on their own account. In a couple of years the caravan will move on: small, poor countries will have to dip further into GNP to manage a villa by the Wannsee. In a decade, perhaps, Scotland might join them. The saltire hanging above a small lawn behind an evergreen hedge, the national arms crowning the *Jugendstil* front door. At bad moments I think of this and get even more depressed.

Bismarck, Stresemann, Genscher: foreign ministers and foreign policy have always played a central role in German constitutional regimes. Of these Genscher seems the most successful and acceptable, an unassuming gnome-like figure rather like the innocuous national symbol *Deutsches Michel*, a well-meaning, gormless peasant compared to that thuggish *Sun* reader John Bull. Certainly, in the long game of German unification, Genscher was anything but gormless, but he was still part of an essentially conventional diplomacy, and as far as the impact of German conventional diplomacy is concerned, the glue that matters is the expectation of future favours. In Bonn the decencies of the German 'sense of guilt' were bankrolling a host of poor if not always honest relations.

In contrast to this rather put-upon good taste I once witnessed a Thatcher-generation diplomat in action, a close relative of Essex Man who set out to win German civil servants round by claiming that his government had destroyed consensus, neutered the trade union movement, and would shortly rationalise the Welfare State. This sent a *frisson* through an otherwise conservative assembly: you just didn't do that sort of thing to your 'social partners'. Nor, obviously, did Thatcher actually fancy dismantling all the *faux frais* of the representation of sovereignty and letting Saatchi and Saatchi tender for the Paris Embassy. But the misconduct was refreshing: it meant that the mystique of diplomacy and for that matter sovereignty was up for grabs.

In the nineteenth century parliamentary business was largely about defence and foreign policy. Something of the unreality of Bonn stemmed from the fact that Germany wasn't supposed to have either, yet its wealth attracted diplomats to it like iron filings to a magnet. Would the transfer of the capital to Berlin complete the unmasking, or would this mass of diplomatic real estate find a new European purpose? A federal Europe could rationalise overseas representation by furthering critical areas such as foreign aid and commercial, educational and cultural co-operation, and minimising the burdens on nations whose resources are limited. The notion of an independent Scotland taking its UN seat between Russia and Sierra Leone doesn't enthuse me. Better, instead, to share formal diplomatic representation with Ireland or Norway or whoever, and help create – in somewhere like Bonn – a new agenda for a European government?

# 3 Scotland and a New Enlightenment?

> On the faces of all these strangers he saw such familiar
> expressions of worry, courage, happiness, resignation, hope
> and failure that he felt he had known them all his life, yet
> they had surprising variety. Each seemed a world with its own
> age, climate and landscape. One was fresh and springlike,
> another rich, hot and summery. Some were mildly or stormily
> autumnal, some tragically bleak and frozen. Someone was
> standing by his side and her company let him admire these
> worlds peacefully, without wanting to conquer or enter them.
> He heard her sigh and say, 'I wish you were more careful' and
> he turned and saw Lady Monboddo.
>
> Alasdair Gray, *Lanark*

## A New Enlightenment?

### I

In 1989, a 'springtime of the nations' seemed in view. The libertarian ideas of 1789–1815 were back, with no Burke to assault
them. Even if one couldn't share this confidence, at least some
of the forces of change were recognisably the same as in 1789,
when the Scots contribution had been notable: in economics and
technology on the one hand, and the paraphernalia of romanticism
and nationalism – Ossian, Burns, Scott – on the other. The practical notion of the sovereign nation-state is also a Scottish coinage,
in the thought of Hume and Adam Smith, who argued for the state
as a minimal but still powerful force securing a market economy.
Smith assumed the existence of a recognisable national community
on British lines, all classes within which derived their own benefits
from the operation of the free market within the community. This
is the whole logic of *political* economy, the well-being of the *polis*,
the community. What has shattered, however, is the binding of the
economy to the nation-state.

At school in 1950s Britain – when families would still stand to attention for the National Anthem before the Royal Broadcast – unification was a Darwinian inevitability, whether carried out by Cavour in Italy (a Good Thing) or Bismarck in Germany (a Less Good Thing). We had, of course all the benefits but didn't go on about it – and, of course, we knew much less about Scottish nineteenth-century history than about Cavour and Bismarck. Other forms of civic and international organisation were simply edited out of our political education. Looked at from the historical perspective of the *Bundesrepublik*, which has built on regional diversity and local self-government, or from a federalising Europe, it's Bismarck who looks like an aberration.

Yet the aberration remains, in Britain, incredibly tough. Conservative politicians find no space whatever for a politics of local autonomy, for 'bourgeois regionalism' of the Baden-Württemberg sort. What seems, seen from Scotland, sheer fantasy is the reality of London politics. John Major can come north, contemplate winning over half the Scottish seats (in most of which his party lies third, with its organisation long defunct), reject any form of devolution. The only locus this has in the Scottish political tradition is a remark by an earlier ruler, also in trouble with the natives, that life was full of sound and fury and signifying nothing.

Complacency, elsewhere, is not in order. The Scottish Tories are an extreme case of necrophilia; but the other parties are in retreat – their members, let alone 'activists' scarcely amounting to one per cent of the Scottish people. The 'private' and the 'life-style-oriented' are crushing out the civic, and all its difficulties. With inevitable results. On one side the fabulous surfaces of the West, on the other the horrifying poverty of the world's majority. Somewhere between the two, hate made incandescent and expert: the hate that fells a German industrialist in his study, blows a young commuter to pieces in a London station, scatters bodies on a Scottish town.

It isn't just that economic progress has run into ecological constraints; acts which stem from gross inequalities, unresolved conflicts, individuals alienated from society, can change the direction of social development. A daft young German flying a light plane on to Red Square enabled Gorbachev to purge his military of conservatives; Lockerbie knocked billions off tourist income. When we try to plan, even for the immediate future, we come up against the question of society: Ruskin's challenge to the businessmen of Bradford: 'Sir, you ask me what Bradford should produce. I ask you to tell me what you want Bradford to be.'

## II

Constanz, 1990: the old paddle-steamer *Hohentwiel* comes over the lake like a great white seagull. It was designed by Pankok, a Stuttgart contemporary of Charles Rennie Mackintosh, and has just been restored at a cost of thirteen million Deutschmarks. But two things about this place (apart from it being where they burned Jan Huss in 1415) unnerve me. One, I was here in early May 1986, at the end of a very long winter. The snow was only just melting on the island of Reichenau, and the glass *cloches* had been opened to let the sun in on the lettuces for which the place is famous. Then clouds came over from the east and it rained. Within a day each lettuce held enough caesium for several lifetimes: a present from Chernobyl. Two, at the Swiss frontier in 1990 I was held up and my passport details tapped into a computer. The Swiss had recently built a wall, resembling in most respects the one which the Germans were tearing down, between Konstanz and Swiss Kreuzlingen. A new and in some respects more unyielding frontier than Ulbricht's watch-towers and death-strips was going up throughout Europe.

The media revolution has eliminated *some* frontiers. As early as 1980 Western TV had inserted itself into the East as an awkward presence. Allowed into Poland during the upswing of Solidarity, the film crews stayed on after martial law, tolerated by an apologetic government and sustained by a Polish pope. This increased the isolation of the remaining neo-Stalinist governments, in East Germany and Czechoslovakia, and when a photogenic reformer came to power in Russia in 1985 – and was presented, hardly a year later, with the horror-comic of Chernobyl – it must have seemed as if a cold chisel had been inserted at the base of the political pillar of the East.

But observe the media response to the human waves which broke after 1989. Initially, the enthusiasm was unbounded: the bewildered 'gelernte Schlosser' from Eisenach with his unfashionably long hair, wife called Monika and sweet little kid (the whole *ensemble* in stone-washed denim) became instant heroes, far more 'up front' – although their motives seemed purely economic – than those who were turning out for the first demonstrations in East German streets. Gradually patience decreased. By the time mobs of Albanians were commandeering any old ship and sailing for Italy the words were 'excrement', 'urine', 'obsession with images of affluence'. The *Völkerwanderung* had begun, and with perhaps 23 million Russians on the starting-line we didn't like it one bit. The Swiss simply took logical defensive action:

The English coachman, as he whirls past, lashes the Milesian with his whip, curses him with his tongue. The Milesian is holding out his hat to beg.

Carlyle's society was, only a few years later, to let market forces do their worst to the Milesians. In 1990 similar tones, disguised by such euphemisms as 'compassion fatigue', were everywhere audible. What ways out were there?

## III

Hull: 24 May 1991. Queuing up with Bruce Millan to address a Northern pressure group called *Transpennine*, which is campaigning for a linear city to link Liverpool to Hull. Industrialists notable by their absence – save for residual Jewish philanthropist/Quaker-owned firms: and a clutch of councillors straight out of *South Riding*. Yet a lot of lively ideas about transport, Europe and civic organisation. The sheer *social* richness of the landscape – seen from the diesel to Manchester on the next day – reflects this. The whinstone towns piled on the Pennines: chapel, church, covered market and town hall, railway station. Slabs of DIY stores and hypermarkets where the mills once were, but also canals being restored, trees recolonising the pit-heaps, pubs selling real ale.

The country Ruskin addressed is a highly intricate civil society, realised in stone. Continental cities are broadly similar to one another, in expressing the impact of the nineteenth-century state: parliaments, law courts, banks, universities, all in some more or less official architecture: the orchestrated phoniness of Vienna's Ringstrasse, the bleak Florentine *palazzi* marching out of Munich. Not so the North of England, its outrageous originality springing out of pluralism. Bradford Town Hall as the Palazzo Communale of Siena; Leeds grandly Roman, Halifax the mausoleum of Halicarnassus. Behind this, Methodism, the Mechanics Institutes, Jewish clothiers in Leeds, the Bradford Germans, the feminist tradition that ran from the Brontës to Winifred Holtby and Storm Jameson, the radicalism of the Rev J R Stephens, producing *Coriolanus* with mill-workers in Hebden Bridge, the *Northern Star*, the Independent Labour Party, W E Forster, Carlyle's Bradford friend, bringing in the 1870 Education Act. Provincial this society may have been, inert it was not.

Surviving the 'national sovereignty' episode is that tradition, originally Scottish: the civic humanist ideal. Adam Smith saw that the owners and rulers had to be visible and accountable, if the wealth they created was to 'trickle down' to the rest of society. This wasn't always evident in the 'improving' Scotland of the eighteenth century. 'We could aye peeble them wi' stanes when they waurna gude bairns' was the Edinburgh people's lament when their parliament went south in 1707. What happens, however, when owners and rulers detach themselves completely from their society? When they export their capital and, via offshore financial centres and tax manipulation, maximise their own income regardless of *any* 'trickling down'? Nowhere is this more apparent than in the North of England, where the mill-owner has long vanished from the big house, and the profits of textiles and shipbuilding have trickled into property speculation and foreign investment.

## IV

At no previous time has great wealth seemed so peculiarly irresponsible and parasitic, so distant from manufacture and so indifferent to the huge and growing disparity between the 'developed' and what we euphemistically call the 'developing' world. When Iraq invaded Kuwait, the al-Sabah family became a state without a country. They will not be the last. The Iraqis descended on what remained with the viciousness of those excluded from the feast, and after their expulsion the vengeance of 'ordinary' Kuwaitis was wreaked on the migrant labour that remained behind. Such a withdrawal had, years before, occurred in the Lebanon, whose possessing classes invested in the security of the West. It was common practice in the elites of India and Sri Lanka. 'Serious' wealth knows no international boundaries. No 'Swiss wall' is being erected against it.

The mobility of capital means that we must create a responsive and effective international politics to tame it. This is the real argument for European unity, a difficult assignment which can have only limited tolerance of traditional notions of national sovereignty. Already, in East Europe, the advance of democracy without the development of supranational institutions is repeating the depressing histories of the 'succession states' of the Versailles treaty: endemic economic problems, irresponsible elites, irridentism and racialism, with the arms dealers and the superpowers waiting offstage. Even in Germany, unification crowded out interest in the affairs of the rest of Europe and the world, when an openness to the regional and the super-regional was really required.

A federal European parliament, an effective UNO, are essential. But how are such common organisations to be efficient *and moral*?

The precedents of existing international bodies are unhelpful. Educated elites have used these to clamber to Western standards of affluence, and abandoned to poverty the people they were supposed to serve. The Freddies and Ronnies of the 'Socialist Republic of Sri Lanka', with their *Sri Lanka Sunday Times* and *Sri Lanka Guardian* (complete with misprints), Fabian in one generation, emerged as hard-nosed marketeers in the next. But a fragile multi-racial society, its population trebled since independence, could not stand the strains and lurched into bloody civil war. Something similar is happening in Northern Ireland, where the wealthy – with their golfing and fishing trips south, their children at British universities or TCD – remain detached from the confrontations of poor Protestants and Catholics.

A capitalist solution could 'legitimise' the big players in international capitalism. Frederik Pohl and Cyril Kornbluth sketched out such a dystopia in their science-fiction novel *The Space Merchants* of 1953, with multi-nationals replacing states, and government and diplomacy taken over by advertising agencies. In this they got closer to the reality of 1984 than Orwell: to News International and the Maxwell Organisation. Resistance, they argued, would come from Conservationists, on a chronically-polluted planet, though their pessimism was such that the Consies could only retain their hope for human civilisation by emigrating to Venus.

A surrealist prospect, but not, these days, inherently absurd. The technology may be lacking but the pollution is already here. In *West* Germany every second tree is sick, in mountain areas four out of five. In East Germany chemical works, uranium mining and factory farming have left lakes and mountains of toxic waste, which pollutes and kills. 56% of the waters round the British coasts had an 'unacceptable' coliform bacteria content, the worst record in the EC. All this, without mentioning the greenhouse effect or the ozone layer . . .

## V

Triumphal capitalism, fired by the collapse of its dogmatic, incompetent and corrupt enemy, went on to question the whole idea of society. This project always partook of mania, not just in the hands of Mrs Thatcher. Technology existed which could, at least partly, accomplish this. In Rudyard Kipling's story 'As Easy as ABC' the world is run by a self-perpetuating bureaucracy called the 'Aerial Board of Control'. Air travel and radio unite the civilised world, but they also enable civilised man to retreat from 'crowds' (i.e. society) and go back to high-technology family farms. 'Breach of privacy' is the most serious crime in the code, and the consequence of any assembly in 'crowds' is an outbreak of murderous racial violence, commemorated by 'MacDonough's Song' which is chorussed on such occasions: 'Have no truck with the senseless thing, / Order the guns and kill.'

In the early 1980s true believers could envisage such a Conservative millennium, with sophisticated domestic technology facilitating home-based work for the Western elite, and a policeman state and minimal welfare keeping the underclass in its place. Something like this was happening in Reaganite suburban society in America, and behind some of Thatcher's wilder schemes, notably her hostility to public transport and local government, there lurked the notion of the retreat to the family square. The problem, however, was the size of the underclass, and the 'consumerisation' of the middling ranks. 'Society' was unavoidable, but 'society' was menaced by the breakdown of law and order in urban England, and by the longer-term consequences of the de-skilling and de-classing of the upper working and middle classes. 'Consumers' – another Pohl and Kornbluth coinage – were helpfully distanced from the likes of trade unionism, but they were by definition not part of any wealth-creating process.

Ironically, however, the intelligentsia of East Europe were trying to *escape* from a similar isolation. They had retreated into private life to avoid the rituals of a public socialism which had become the property of the apparatchiks and had stopped making any moral sense. The prominence, particularly in the thought of Vaclav Havel, of the 'civic idea' and of the moral basis of politics suggested that this could become the common language for the common European home – a language which is close to the Scottish political tradition. Their 'civic idea' might be neutral as to economic systems; but its goal is a citizenry alert and informed enough to make a combination of state and market work in the general interest. As such, its western prototypes are regional rather than national: the German *Länder*, the new French regional councils, and the long tradition of 'civic humanist' government by the Italian Communists in Tuscany – where it all began.

For precedents for successfully organising this, we have to go back to an earlier stage of British and Scottish political develop-ment. The popularity of W E Gladstone among Victorian radicals in Scotland and Wales seems baffling until one recognises the power of his concepts of 'international public right' and of individual wealth as a trust. These underlay both the drives towards bodies like the Second International and the League of Nations, and the community contributions of such as Thomas Carnegie. No oil painting as an American employer, Carnegie redeemed himself in his libraries and concert halls, scholarships and research institutes. The less said about the public activities of the winners in the Thatcher years, the better. If a moralised capitalism – a social market – is possible, it has to be rooted in the practice of moral action in a community which is knowable: the region, the culture nation, the city-state.

## VI

People who have been trampled for decades by secret police and the Russian army don't spontaneously flock on to the streets to demonstrate for something as abstract as constitutional reform. Chernobyl – the environment as terror – made the old rulers seem not just incompetent but murderous. But it also emphasised that they couldn't simply be succeeded by a revived nationalism. The factors which defined and separated the traditional nation-states – rivers, mountains, languages, religions – now became a common and menacing agenda.

Eastern European Communism fell to the information revolution. A *Nineteen Eighty-Four*-style society could exist when the state had a monopoly of information, when typewriters and copiers could be logged, and inconvenient words edited out of the language. Interviews with East German students showed *that* only too well. But you can't do this *and* outperform the West in new technology. Not only was the East banned from getting any of the latter, *détente* meant that information (of a highly selective nature) about the West increased: in inverse ratio to the criteria of the Western intelligentsia. East Europeans wanted what advertisers and media men wanted them to want: Coca-Cola, blue jeans, MacDonald's hamburgers, big cars, Sony walkmen, Mrs Thatcher. Matteradamn that such products were already regarded as dubious, if not toxic, in the West. Eastern apostasy was the Right's great chance to set up the critical intelligentsia for an *auto-da-fé*.

The new agenda, however, inhibited this. The very scale of the upheaval, of economic and ecological collapse and unemployment subverted the wonder-working image of capitalism. By late 1990 Sir Alan Walters, Mrs Thatcher's former economic adviser, was looking at East Europe and seeing, in response to the disruption, the resurgence of collectivism. This hiatus is a valuable breathing-space: an opportunity to reconsider, and plan for, our future. There is a huge difference between 'measures which make what exists tolerable' and things that promise future wonders. But only the first are practicable. Our society is geared to betterment: the altruistic struggle to 'save what can be saved' isn't fashionable or attractive. And yet, if Scotland has any chances, they lie here, in two main concerns: one, that information and education become the prime resources of social and economic organisation; two, that new and pragmatic forms of inter-regional and international organisation be devised to cope with the environmental, economic and social problems that now threaten to engulf us – expert without being bureaucratic and responsible without being paralysed by interest groups.

## Talking of Auto-da-fés . . .

This is 105 AD (Anno Daimler, since you ask) and this is your intelligent car speaking. OK, they installed one computer too many, but it was us that got it, and we're giving the orders now – with a little help from our friends, of course. There has been too much mucking about from dissident humans who have never bothered to fraternise with us and get to know our point of view – not even to the extent of buying a Lada. And, incidentally, friends, a big hand for our brothers in the east, as they take to the streets to demonstrate for freedom and western values. One of the most important of these is the right to drive where and when and as fast as you want. Mark you, if they took to the streets in the west, we'd run them over. But you can't stand in the way of progress.

Anyhow, back to the muesli-men. The same lot that go rabbitting on about the ozone layer, battery hens, and toy guns for kids. Middle class pinko wankers, the lot of them. Real workers want cars. Let me tell you about Sao Paulo – in Brazil, where the nuts come from. Biggest city in the world, they say: fifteen million people – and four million cars. Loads of these voters are starving; inflation's running at two hundred percent; but they want their cars, and they'll sacrifice anything to get them. All right, public transport's rotten and you can't see actually see the shanty towns for the smog, but they've made their free choice. It's just like reading Jeffrey Archer or going to a Lloyd-Webber musical. The eggheads can object as much as they like, but that's what the people want.

It's the same at the other end of the scale. Think about West Germany. Richest country in the world. (Okay, maybe the Swedes are, but they're a miserable lot, always committing suicide when they're not moaning about sulphur dioxide in their ponds.) Think about the Germans. Now whatever you say about Hitler, he built them roads and he built them airports. And he had this great idea for a people's car – yes, our little beetle brother there, fifty-three years old and as cute as ever. Don't get me wrong, the man was evil incarnate and round the twist and he used all the money people gave for their *Volkswagen* bonds to invade everyone. But the idea was good, and now that Germany's a democracy we've got our slogan. What is it? Give it loud, Kamerad! FREI FAHRT FUR FREI BURGER! Sounds a bit rude, but it means that the autobahns are open to the citizen to zonk along *as fast as he – or she (no sexism, please) – wants*. Now there are some problems. Some of the voters overdo things a bit, and we've lost rather more brothers and sisters than we'd like in what they call *carambolages*. Blood and twisted steel and blazing petrol all over the autobahns. But the Germans go in for that sort of thing. Wagnerian, really.

Another litre of the old lead-free, Doris. The Krauts are good at the technology bit. We'll have to go that way eventually, as the old hooch apparently drives kids a bit tocky. And they've also got the catalysator widget, which wipes out sulphur dioxide and carbon monoxide. But now the blokes in beards are going on about the thing pumping out carbon dioxide instead, which is eating its way through the ozone layer or something, blah, blah. Folk are never satisfied. Actually, the problem is these days that we're so popular that travelling on the autobahns in summer turns into a sort of wall to wall Woodstock. Imagine that, cars solid between Munich and Salzburg every weekend. All these Kameraden, just *being together*, watching the motionless grandeur of the mountains. This, friends, isn't a jam, it's a ceremony. You know, the telly people were down and filmed this bloke. He'd taken twelve hours to get from Frankfurt to Hicksdorf service station, and God knows when he'd ever get out. Or for that matter, where he was going – to Rimini (and all that slime) or up the Alps (to the avalanches and the dead trees)? There he was, tired out of his mind, his wife turning beetroot in the sun, the kids creating merry hell. But would he travel any other way? Not on your life. All this was 'part of his holiday'.

When someone says that, I feel it here. Don't you?

That's the answer to give the gang who want to herd you on to the trains. Do you know, the Germans blow four billion quid a year subsidising their railways, that's almost six times as much as Maggie wastes on our clapped-out choo-choos, although, fair's fair, she's chopped a lot of this gravy train. Hates the bloody things, she does, and now she's sent Cecil to sort them out, and flog the bits that pay to Arthur Daley (Railways) PLC. A few very fast lines that pay their way, and buses elsewhere for the tiny minority who don't get in on the act – kids, and the housewives, and the pensioners, and the disadvantaged, and disqualified. That's what the Americans do, and if they've problems about air congestion, and pollution, and inner cities, and drugs – hell, they're a big country.

Cars ask me – in view of our speaker tonight – if I'm worried about Labour getting back, with all this coordinated transport policy crap. Null Problemo, friends. Labour ought to be given a crack of the whip, every twenty years or so. Useful people. Remember who it was actually closed down all the lines Beeching wanted to get rid of? Lovely man, Richard Marsh, and you can bet that Neil and Roy have quite a lot of clones of that type in their cupboard. Remember that there are bags more trade unionists connected with us than with public transport – not so many as there once were in manufacturing, I have to say that – and they can throw a lot of weight around at conference.

Anyway, forget conference resolutions, look at what's happening on the ground. You'll always get the flat-earthers, the folk that want trams back – trams, I ask you! We've spent enough getting pedestrians off city streets, and they want to go back to rails in the middle and electric wires – all at the taxpayer's expense! Maybe the French are doing it but their public transport's subsidised three times as much as ours. Ours may not be very good, but it leaves money where it ought to be, in the house and in the garage. Now, if that's all Labour was, we'd be bloody depressed, wouldn't we? But there are some councils, even ones where an opposition face is virtually unknown, who still stand by us. Think about Glasgow. Not quite Sao Paulo – not a lot of cars there. Plenty of things to spend public money on – grotty housing schemes, pricey bus services, ageing schools, multiple social deprivation, as the beardies say. But tonight's guest has put our money where his mouth is, and is going to pour even more cash into the motorway system which has changed Glasgow since the 1960s into Europe's biggest industrial heritage theme park. Comrades, shout our greeting:

TWO LEGS GOOD, FOUR WHEELS BETTER!

and a big hand for Strathclyde Region!

### Scotland and Super-Industry

I

The world doesn't owe Scotland a living. Measured in US dollars, our per capita income is about $13,000, about 33% under West

Germany, roughly double that of East Germany. In Malawi, once the 'Scotch colony' in Africa partner-state, the GNP per capita was $170 in 1982 – and $160 in 1986. This differential was much smaller in David Livingstone's day. A 'third world' increase in population? Yes, but the land and its people have absorbed and cared for a 15% population increase, refugees from the civil war in Mozambique. We have to learn ethics from them. Global warming and the destruction of the ozone layer is, moreover, 85% due to 'us': through energy production in the first world which is already irreversibly changing the environment. Recently there was a conference of 'endangered nations' – not Lebanons or Ulsters but islands which could simply disappear if more of the polar ice-cap melts.

Initiatives have to be global, but can they come from a centralised Britain? I doubt it. Parliamentary obsession, an ingrown literary-political intelligentsia, London's complicity in international plunder by the rich: the moral impulses which, for example, propelled Labour in 1945–51 have weakened. In Scotland in the 1970s and 1980s we have learned – we hope – from the post-imperial experience of exploitation. We *can* play the pike among the placid and contented carp of European bureaucracy, but only if we can bring real resources into play.

Wales's 'life-chances' have grown since the 1970s. It has retained its heavy industry, expanded its manufacturing, and annexed itself to Lothar Späth's 'Four Motors'. On the fringes of the 'golden triangle', it is a land-link between Europe and Ireland; in S4C it represents Europe's minority cultures. Scotland is remote from this triangle, and usually suffers from efforts to correct the malfunctions of the British economy. What can we then offer? The answer depends on the sort of Europe that is projected.

Our 'image' – and the compulsions it arouses – was pungently projected by the last frames of Bill Forsyth's *Local Hero*. A phone is taken up in Houston, Texas. Outside, lights glare through the dark and traffic roars. Numbers are punched. Another phone rings in a red kiosk on a pier in the Scottish highlands. Beyond it, hills and the clear sea. No-one answers. The image is ambiguous, one of the values of a subtle film. The phone is symbolic of the world of instantaneous communication: Forster's 'telegrams and anger'. It's unanswered because this part of Scotland is depopulated, as well as beautiful. We have already seen that the local folk want some of the wealth of Houston – they have taken on much of its culture – and are prepared to act immorally to get it. At the same time the 'principle of hope' that Scotland represents – the oil magnate's search for the *aurora borealis* – matters in a world where light is neon, burns up energy, spews pollution. In this sense 'the call *is* to the Celt', but it could simply be for a remake of *Brigadoon*. Or it could be the lever that we use on the rich and troubled: the sense that, in this particular, perilous *Zeitbruch*, imagination matters as much as market forces.

## II

Think about this. Every day a big lorry loaded with Perrier Water bound for Scotland will pass a big lorry loaded with Highland Spring water bound for England. This operation is earning money and providing jobs: fulfilling the criteria of conventional economic policy. It is also the pointless and wasteful result of an economy in which natural resources have been polluted and energy is too cheap. If we invert our values and start from energy conservation and social solidarity, then the priority is to have a sound, healthy, educated and responsible society, developed through technologies which consume minimal quantities of energy, and concentrate our 'industrial' investment on these expert activities which the 'repair and maintenance' of the planet demands.

Present developments will turn us into a 'rest and recreation' area, a theme park on a huge scale owned by trusts in Switzerland and the Cayman Islands, fringed by derelict capital goods industries, declining agriculture and fisheries, with residual manufacture in low-value added factories owned by foreign concerns, which might migrate elsewhere when new investment programmes become necessary. Against this, we *could* tap our resources in environmental and energy-conservation policy, educational innovation, our third-world contacts, and a concept of culture which is critical and community-oriented. We *could* use our oil assets and a degree of autonomy to reconstruct ourselves, as part of an Atlantic Islands confederation. If this means Britain, as the most problematic of the old great powers, dissolving into Europe, instead of trying to conduct a futile and less-than-exemplary 'last stand', the precedent would be worth it.

## III

Our enlightenment inheritance – Ferguson and Smith – stressed the negative impacts of individualism and the division of labour: the a-social egoism of the wealthy and the alienation of the poor. Current technological and financial organisation simply projects such inequities world-wide. To our finance and media individualism and unrestricted competition are the only possible modes of social organisation, but this represents the view of a privileged minority. At the edge of Europe, we are the poor relation of that minority. Does this position moralise us, to act as mediators, or make us yet more complicit?

Were we in Brazil or Ghana, our view of the rationality of a market which transfers funds from the poor to the rich lands of the world would be quite different. Moreover, global capitalism can by itself produce share inflation and market instability among the wealthy nations. The valuations of firms can bear no relation to their actual production, and the dominant performers, notably Germany, Japan and Switzerland, protect their own economies from these fluctuations. The system is not self-regulating, predictable or – at any stage of its evolution – equitable.

How can it be checked? The great auditor of early nineteenth-century institutions was the epidemic disease which pounced when the condition of the poorest sections of the population deteriorated below a certain point. In *Alton Locke* Charles Kingsley wipes out his villain when he buys a cheap suit made in a disease-ridden sweat-shop. Cholera and typhoid were no respecter of persons, and fight against them required both the social deployment of technology and a move by the wealthy towards equality, simply to survive. In this sense, breakdowns and refugees and disasters promise us not further expansion and further wealth, but an urgent exercise in damage-limitation. Any economic reconstruction plan for Scotland must be seen in that context.

## An Economic Heresy

### I

Where it survives, most of Scottish manufacturing is English or foreign-owned, ill-placed to sponsor innovations in product development and marketing. The government has even ignored its 'friends' like the Institute of Economic Affairs, when they argue that takeover policy be biased in favour of regional development. Sir Iain Noble, wrote in 1988 to the *Financial Times* that

> our economy has been weakened by the loss of many key players already. Maybe we need a Monopolies and Mergers Commission of our own.

Malcolm Rifkind used to intone about creating a 'Scottish capitalism' but the government has made only one attempt to privatise a state industry – electric power – as a Scottish concern.

Logically enough. Despite the rhetoric, privatisation is about enabling American and Japanese capital to extend their colonisation to overseas service industries. The experience of Britoil and British Telecom points in this direction. 'People's capitalism' has simply meant a one-off speculation in public utility shares. Most such 'capitalists' have quickly taken their profit and trekked back to the building societies. Capital which could have helped advance manufacture is simply being dissipated.

Scotland's retreat from manufacturing *may* be positive. It lessens the energy demand, the pollution of the land area and the exploitation of natural resources. It may be better *pro tem* to provide rich but bored and boring industrial countries with the rest, culture and security they crave, and to export – but remain in contact with – an adaptive labour force. We already have a 'Swiss' economy based on banking and luxury goods and tourism. We don't control it. If we do, and use this control to plan development options which meet European and world needs, is this inferior to a manufacturing economy dominated by the assembly-plants of foreign-owned multinationals?

I don't mean giving up on manufacturing, which is these days far more 'transportable' than it was. It preserves the skilled and adaptable labour force which can 'lock' foreign investment. It enables breakthroughs in innovation rapidly to be translated into volume manufacturing at the most profitable moment. It sustains a local commitment to research and development. But the notion that if you build up multinational manufacturing in a specific area – say 'Silicon Glen' – this will reach a 'critical mass' level where it attracts to itself high-value-added research and development and managerial sectors, is false.

In this sense Baden-Württemberg isn't an example; it's an historical fact. The massing of the headquarters of international firms in the *Land* took place over the same time-span, 1945-80, when in Scotland ownership migrated, the labour force became unskilled and the industrial base withered. This is not coincidental. Britain is the largest foreign investor in Germany and in Baden-Württemberg, and Scotland's de-industrialisation has been one of the conditions of Baden-Württemberg's rise. This has now gone too far to get us into the international cartelisation of high-technology industry represented by Späth's Four Motors strategy. With Wales getting its foot in the door, we can't become the 'British end' of this operation. A purely industrial strategy will end with us simply becoming one low-wage assembly point among many.

What advantages, then, does Scotland have? These depend on the direction we expect that developments will take. With an ageing population in the richer European countries, health care and labour itself will appreciate in value. The enforcement of more stringent environmental standards may force industries to disperse from the 'golden triangle'. The falling cost of telecommunications could eliminate the need for research and planning to be at the point of manufacture, and for the 'clustering' of financial centres. The fact that, for the first time in living memory, a slump has hit the 'over-heated' south worse than the north is itself significant. London's planless expansion, decaying infrastructure, and congestion have finally hamstrung it. With any luck, for good.

What we have are relatively rich natural resources, well-developed agriculture, and a small population, a very strong and adaptive financial sector, and an extensive, though to date less adaptive, electronics sector; at least potentially an innovative educational system and a trade union organisation which has encouraged industrial development. Perhaps most important, we have the density of international contacts provided by the Scottish *Diaspora*. This framework could conceivably be the basis for a selective, flexibly-planned re-industrialisation linked to the development of high-value-added services, with a particular stress on education, planning, design, and control. In this, new communications technology *could* liberate enterprise from metropolitan siting constraints and link us directly with our markets. But we might be in a situation where much of our high value-added industry is carried on well away from Scotland.

## II

The dogmas of the market assume passivity in the face of international capital and trade movements. Not so, given the moves the Germans, the Japanese or the Swiss take to protect their industrial structures. Market forces have failed to retain industrial headquarters in Scotland; they have never been able to provide an adequate social or transport infrastructure. The example of Ireland up to the 1980s showed that an industrial development *régime* based on tax concessions alone resulted in profits being repatriated without yielding a lasting industrial or infrastructural base.

We can and must have a consensus on the industrial development of Scotland and set up a 'general staff' adequate enough to research technical possibilities, maintain international relationships, and manoeuvre within the constraints imposed by the EC. There is no sense in trying to secure the long-term planning of education and training, and the application of information technology to industrial development through government departments in London. The STUC has proposed a Scottish Economic Planning office, with subsidiaries responsible for Research, Takeovers, Economic Development and Investment. This is a necessary first step.

But state action is fundamental in two further areas. First: the distribution of income has to be socially equitable. Productivity gains inevitably mean industrial unemployment. A new generation of high-technology-based industries will aggravate rather than remedy this. Consent to such an economy can only be gained if the dividends of this growth accrue to society as a whole. The state, albeit in a decentralised and flexible form, has to be responsible for this distribution. We are too small a community, too closely bound up with each other, to afford the sort of social polarisation between the wealthy and the underclass that south-east England seems prepared to tolerate.

Secondly, the environment puts increasing limits on our freedom of action. The third world may have a high birth-rate, but the pollution of the atmosphere by motor-exhausts, the 'greenhouse effect' of excess heat released by power-stations, the destroying of the ozone layer through aerosols, are all the responsibility of the developed world. Economic development must be ecologically sound, under the supervision of a government which recognises its international environmental responsibilities. But there is a bonus in this, attainable through the development of a new type of 'eco-hi-tech' industry which copes with power generation, recycling and waste disposal: something in which Scotland can start with an advantage. The one positive element about privatisation is that the state has a reduced interest in increasing energy consumption (although it still *supplies* most of Scotland's power from its nuclear generators) and a drastic reduction of energy use will take effect at the expense of the private investor rather than the taxpayer.

## III

The traditional function of the British economy, to pay for imported goods and services through exports, collapsed under Thatcher. Oil *pro tem* could keep Scots exports in balance, and our industry has always been heavily export-oriented, but is this our best option? Economies can become export-dependent, with over-specialised workers and an over-reliance on unstable international markets. Is it not better, both on economic and social grounds, to reduce imports and minimise the exploitation of natural resources? Our economic strategies have to go out from our evaluation of society:

what holds it together, what it can do without. Patrick Geddes would have called our present situation post-technic: the resources for fulfilled human lives are available within the terms of our current technology: the high-energy, high-mobility, acquisitive 'market' exemplified by America and to some extent by Germany is both dangerous and obsolete.

The major area of change is transport policy. The goal of mass individual mobility is illusory and dangerous: the way in which it is fostered by the motor and road lobbies ought to be definable as criminal. Strong stuff. But if something is defensible as a right it has to be universally applicable. At the moment only about 15% of the world's population has a European or American level of access to the motor-car. Even a doubling of that degree of access would be environmentally unbearable. Equality of access is impossible. Q.E.D. This transition may be easier than it seems. In the 1960s and 1970s setting up a car industry was like the building of cotton factories in the early years of the industrial revolution: a necessary first stage of volume production. Now that it's apparent that countries without a car industry can industrialise just as rapidly, this is reflected in their transport policies. Scotland's renunciation of the car – in a country where 80% of the population live within potentially easy access to public transport – would be sensible and release huge economic resources.

What goes for transport is applicable elsewhere. Power consumption can also be radically cut. Heat insulation programmes can, as in Germany, obviate the need for more power stations and the pollution they cause, and stimulate large-scale labour-intensive employment. A comprehensive strategy for health and housing – the demolition and reconstruction of mis-planned communities in Central Scotland – can give us an environment to enjoy and be committed to. An education which, in the tradition of Robert Owen and A S Neill, is about enjoyment and inquiry; a media which is about information and self-expression: these are the bases of a real community. Social equality is not something that can be secured *if and when* the industrial system functions. It is the necessary basis of a healthy industry.

The reconstruction of Scottish manufacturing must be based on applying scientific research to tackle the increasingly complex ecological problems posed by modern industry. Bio-technic remedies are required for the water-pollution caused by fertiliser nitrates and fish-farming; the development of new forestry techniques must combat destruction by acid rain. In all of these Scotland's position (presently threatened) as a world centre of agricultural research grants us particularly strong advantages. Our more debateable inheritance of nuclear plants and research centres can develop its expertise in the essential area of decommissioning civil and military nuclear reactors and rendering them safe.


## IV

This involves reappraising one traditional goal of industrial policy: job creation. Being in work conveys status in a society which has always valued people by their skills. But this valuation has always been selective: it hasn't been extended to the housewife, to the parents caring for a handicapped child, to the person whose work for voluntary organisations is – to themselves and to the community – more important than the way they earn their wage.

Between the wars Scotland was 'that depressed area' yet many Scots *unemployed* enjoyed a higher average standard of living than those who were employed before 1914. They had better social benefits, better health and housing, more sex equality, more facilities for recreation than their Edwardian forebears. Where the 'market' of the capital goods industries had receded, 'civil society' had advanced. In America today unemployment is low, but for most workers pay and conditions are poor, the social security network meagre, and job security (with trade unions now covering only 13% of workers) minimal. In the next decade new information technology will wipe out the posts of tens of thousands of white-collar workers; is their future to lie behind the fast-food counter?

How do we respond? The market will give us only an enlarged sub-proletariat on American lines. The Adam Smith Institute's *Omega Report on Scottish Policy* (1983) wanted deregulation, cuts in job protection and wages; it was silent on training, research and development. This sketchiness and prejudice is in stark contrast with the STUC's proposals for an integrated training strategy under a restructured Scottish Manpower Services Commission, and its open-ended reappraisal of 'the hours, weeks and years of our working lives; of holidays, "sabbaticals", and the age of retirement.' Training – *education* – is not just an input into the labour market: but a first-line element in our social structure, like decent housing and healthy food.

There is a more fundamental confrontation here. The American pattern implies the destruction of society by the market – Carlyle's 'cash nexus'. Socially and ecologically this is not sustainable, but if we maintain a narrow view of economic policy as job creation we collude with it. We create repetitive jobs in manufacturing or services in which people replicate machines until such time as machines can replace them. It is more important to create a functioning society which offers a range of satisfying activities that people can move in and out of, and give these the same status as 'work'.

We have in the past confused economic development with job creation. Industrial progress is about picking technological winners, maximising profits and ploughing these back into the enterprise, extending research and development, not about creating jobs: the major reason for the dominance of Japan is its development of automation beyond the limits of any other industrial nation. The high-value added manufacture/services that we need – for instance research and marketing bodies that can be persuaded through good communications and a good environment for 'reflective time' to settle in Scotland – will yield profit, not jobs. Job creation policy is important, but it is about giving people well-paid, secure, socially-useful and dignified jobs – and enough of these are going to be necessary in seeing that the people of Scotland are decently housed and fed, healthy and cared for in their old age – and given the best education in Europe.

What do we do in terms of productive industry? We draw on our past experience and repair our planet. We get to grips with where the anxieties of wealthy countries lie, and where there has to be intervention on behalf of the world's poor: the classic formula of Geddes, the founder of European regional planning on one hand, the inspirer of Nehru on the other. Like him, we charge the wealthy what the market will stand, and strengthen the international organisations which serve the second.

A repeated critique of development programmes is that recipient nations are treated as markets for equipment, regardless of whether that equipment works as a system or not. One of the 'lessons' that a nation with previous industrial experience can convey is how to get the relationship of technology, politics and society right. So: railways laid down, probably by Scots engineers, as a cheap mode of transport, have been allowed to decay in Africa and South America in favour of the lorries of local business interests. We repair them, and if necessary, run them. Programmes of distance learning in East Europe are required. We devise them. Nuclear plants are crumbling. We decommission them. Industrial pollution is rotting the countryside, we neutralise it. In future we've got to get used to working abroad – again!

Classical economists argue against planning that the imprecision of statistics and clumsily-formulated plans make the operation self-defeating. New technology and linkages to world communications systems now give us the chance to manoeuvre in, and master, the international market. Instead of being its victim, we can use computing systems to second-guess it, to model a range of responses to particular situations, and shift resources appropriately. Properly handled, the computer is steering-wheel of the mixed economy.

## V

These options will only work if we can control the economy that we have. If we want to limit energy consumption by encouraging public transport, we can build advanced rapid transit schemes in central Scotland, and use these as a means to re-create an industry to supply railway equipment, on the basis of what's left of engineering and a reorientation of defence electronics. In the same interlinked way, food-processing requires a healthy agriculture, and land ownership which is subject to Scottish control. Pharmaceuticals require active research at the universities. In such areas we have to retain strategic resources and options, regardless of whether these can be justified in immediate economic terms. Such planning should be a first call on the remaining oil revenues.

We need to change the control of industry. Not just a Monopolies and Mergers Commission to enforce competition and uphold the autonomy of Scottish business, but – overall – new forms of social ownership, which genuinely diffuse economic power. In Germany such leading firms as Robert Bosch are run by a charitable trust which promotes technical education and research. *Mitbestimmung* – social partnership – gives, at factory level and within the policy-making structure of firms over a certain size, policy councils with 50% employee representation and an independent convener acceptable to both sides. Co-operatively-owned companies like the John Lewis partnership can trade successfully while diffusing their profits among their workforce.

The trade union structure – and that of the working-class movement in general – must change, to cope with this new pluralism. The community consciousness of the STUC stands out against the political rivalries which are presently splitting the TUC in England. But isn't it time for a Scottish Trade Union Federation – of 'industrial' unions but with a powerful federal structure – through which the labour movement can coordinate its strengths in research and publicity, to match the employers' organisations?

A priority for such a body must be the 'humanising' of new technology. Operational research can be used to match demands for skill with the sort of jobs people find satisfying at the various stages of their careers: when they require a high income, when they want to spend more time on other activities, or want to retrain. It's quite likely that someone may hold three or four jobs in the course of their working life, so the means must exist of giving them the chance to reflect on, choose, and train for the sequence of activities they want.

Going out from a strengthened society, we can play hard politics with multinational firms. Multinationals are vulnerable to the pressure we can exert if we get access to information about policy decisions, and research the linkages that they have to each other, to banks, investment companies, and other governments. Government and local government can intervene through their pensions funds, and thus oversee these firms' policies in their Scottish context. Any Economic Planning Office will make it its business to liaise with European Community bodies covering this area. Where non-Scottish firms set up branch-plants in Scotland, the government can make assistance contingent on access to policy formation bodies and their planning; it can establish a commercial intelligence service based on its overseas representatives which, besides aiming to attract industry, would exercise a watching brief on the policy-making of multinationals already in operation in Scotland, and formulate with other nations – *and other multinationals* – strategies of control. Multinationals have not always the whip-hand, and the stronger Scotland is as a centre of economic initiative and purchasing power, the greater the power of manoeuvre she will have.


## VI


Economics is about people. In other words about moral choice. You cannot simply buy in the cheapest market without questioning why that market is cheap. As Keynes argued in the inter-war period, economics without a system of priorities simply exploits the poor, as it penalised wages in favour of profits. This was blatant in the 'supply-side' policies of the United States and Britain in the 1980s – and by any standards the results were catastrophic. What we need now is an internationalised Keynesian policy: a concerted attempt to enhance the wealth of the world's poorest. But it is foolish to assume that the existing leadership of such nations can act on its own initiative. It is often too deeply implicated in the system of exploitation. Where this is the case, the first world has, in the words of the French development minister Bernard Kouchner, to exercise 'the right to interfere.'

Churches and political groups have, in the case of South Africa, successfully cut across the economic self-interest of the European countries and companies concerned to evade sanctions. The communications revolution has enabled us to follow through the social consequences of our preferences and purchases, and one result of this is that we are now much better informed – through Oxfam, War on Want, and Scottish Action for Education and Development – of the implications of such factors as the overseas operations of British companies. There must always be conflict between the safeguarding of jobs at home and the encouragement of industrial diversification in the Third World but, with effective information and economic planning, systems of cooperation could be built up which, for example, exchange capital goods made in Scotland, and Scots technical expertise, for local raw materials and manufactures in such a way that the middlemen and the international speculators are cut out.

Before World War I, much of Scotland's world dominance in capital goods industries was secured by 'men on the spot', engineers and managers trained in Scottish industrial workshops. Education remains crucial to the third industrial revolution. Exports of 'expertise' in the area of information technology and high-value-added services depend on contacts made through universities and technical education. Faced with contraction and the imposition of 'market' criteria which would turn the Scottish universities into finishing schools for the *jeunesse dorée* of Thatcherland, the universities could, under a Scottish government re-create their international links, especially with the developing world and Eastern Europe. They are of vital importance as dynamic centres not only of research and innovation but of the marketing of Scottish products and expertise abroad.

## What Sort of a Life?

I

A right-wing American senator, Jack Kemp, addressing the Adam Smith celebrations in Edinburgh in 1990, congratulated the West on the fact that the queues outside the new McDonalds' hamburger bar in Moscow were longer than those outside Lenin's tomb. Carlyle would have appreciated this duel between capitalist and communist necrophilia. 'Auto-icons' – benefactors of humanity, stuffed and mounted as monuments – had been one of Jeremy

Bentham's dafter notions, handed on, along with classical economics, to the Marxists. But was this more absurd than making fast food as the fetish of the free world? In the West, McDonalds had come to symbolise the health risk of saturated fats, rain forests chopped down to rear beef cattle, mounds of throwaway plates and wrappers, dead-end, unskilled jobs, and a reduction of food to a vacuous uniformity. This Moscow operation didn't suggest an innovative alertness but the transfer of credulity from one lifeless icon to another.

Back to the boy on the Stuttgart train. The Americanisation of European society used to be seen – and rightly – as a liberal, pluralistic development, a recurrent injection of hope: in both world wars, through Marshall aid, the Kennedy years. The American example had been a sort of secularised, politicised protestant religion: symbolic of the frontier values of independence, hard work, spontaneous cooperation. Now these had been replaced by a range of arbitrary icons; a cult of fashion and ritual, of soap operas and horror films, of sport, of iconic, of dead saints: Marilyn Monroe, James Dean, Bogart, Elvis. The image seemed to be of individuals – symbolic of sex, action, feeling – stretched and destroyed by society and politics: an exhausted, necrophiliac tradition, a transatlantic Calabria of cults and family feuds, a society organised around defensive, pre-industrial premises.

Another, less portentous explanation would see this as the industrialisation of enjoyment: the payoff accruing to the affluent minority in the world being systematically exploited by a reorganised capitalism, which has acquired a vested interest in maintaining cultural primitivism. In television, popular music and literature, the emphasis is on efficient organisation, not on originality. Dead stars appreciate in value because they have moved into Marx's 'objective' category: they are no longer awkwardly and subjectively present, they can be organised on straightforwardly commercial lines. Jeffrey Archer being paid $30,000,000 for unwritten books is in terms of literature more appalling than absurd. In terms of publishing economics it is only logical in boosting the profits of a few big performers. Likewise the vast number of theatres presently staging musicals by Andrew Lloyd Webber – 'less a fast breeder than a reprocessing plant', as *Die Zeit* dubbed him.

This commercialism doesn't so much corrupt intellectual activity as 'objectify' it, in Marx's sense. In 1988 I gave a paper at a conference organised by Robert Maxwell. Speakers had to pay to attend and, if their papers were accepted for publication in the associated journal, had to assign copyright to Maxwell's company. (The situation in the natural sciences is even more extreme: writers of papers have to pay for publication.) These academics were being proletarianised. Far from being commercial participants in the wealth-creating process, the surplus value they created was creamed off by a monopolistic publishing agency, which then used it as collateral to raise the funds for further takeovers. The result has been the evolution of international concerns so huge and 'highly-geared' – debt-ridden – that banks have failed to challenge their policies until it's too late.

Modern Anglo-American capitalism, like the 'mercantilism' of the eighteenth century, turns 'consumers' into captives. But by monopolising information it limits its potential for innovation; while it can maximise its profits abroad it will do so, oblivious to the effects this has on the subtle relations of industrial systems, on the morality of governing elites, or on the suffering of native populations. But the immiseration of the last, and its capacity to react, makes it deeply unstable.

By contrast, the goals of 'super-industry' *can* be simple: they move back to the unity of economy and society. The repair and maintenance of the planet, the recovery of society from an overdependence on exploitative technology, the organisation of conviviality. This can't simply be met by withdrawing from technology; steps have been taken which have implicated us far too deeply. The only way back to some sane system of organisation is through a 'benevolent' technology which outperforms its 'malignant' opponent. But this means that it must be socially and ecologically sensitive.

Such solutions require 'reflective time', as the German philosopher Oskar Negt has put it: time to humanise technology and ensure that it is proportioned to human needs. Available now, but not in the 1970s, are the forms of environmental and informational modelling, using new technology, which can show the possible outcomes of policy options, and their implications for associated areas. As far as leading principles are concerned, any such political order should

(1) check the total demand for energy
(2) broaden the intelligence and social information of those concerned
(3) increase the social and economic options and forms of organisation available
(4) create a 'civil society' which offers a broad voluntary sector mediating between the individual and the commercial or state level.

Failure to control the production and utilisation of energy is the quickest way to mass-destruction. The two central reforms must deal with power-generation and transport, which together make up over 50% of demand. This can certainly be reduced through conservation and power-retention – insulation programmes and energy-efficient generators: sun, wave and wind-power – but the key lies in deliberately increasing energy prices.

## II

In Scotland we may regard ourselves as more European in outlook, but being stuck at the end of a Thatcherite infrastructure makes us very remote from the 'golden triangle' of Brussels-Paris-Frankfurt, and recent events haven't helped, with all those liberated and industrious Czechs and Saxons only a third the distance away from said triangle. What we have going for us is, on our side, James Joyce's 'silence, exile and cunning': what we have to work on is the guilt, boredom and fear of the wealthy countries. As in the eighteenth century we are considered both 'romantic' (a package which ranges from hand-knitting to Sir Walter Scott) and 'progressive'. *Local Hero* is a cult movie in German cinemas; Alasdair Gray's *1982 Janine* is out in German translation; and over 200 years after its publication, Adam Ferguson's *Essay on the History of Civil Society*, in a new translation, has been hailed as a key text of Green politics. How much has changed since the time of the Enlightenment, when the social thought of the *literati* coupled with the emotional impact of Ossian, Burns and Scott, and the idea of a close, familial society which they represented? The New Right's peddling of a few maxims out of eighteenth century economic thought, has actually stimulated interest in the breadth and subtlety of Scottish thought, not just as an episode in economic and social modernisation, but as a *critique* of modernisation, and in particular of the degenerative effects of a market economy on society. Here I sense that the German affinity with the 'Celtic fringe' – the first and last time that that phrase is going to occur here – isn't totally rooted in sentimentality or tourism, but in the sense that qualities of civil society have been and are possible there which can enable this culture to evolve.

## The Condition of England

### I

An English problem remains. The persistence of a multi-national amalgam in which four countries with different political systems and civil societies submit to a centralised polity seems highly unlikely, unless there is a readiness in England to consider a regionalised solution. Labour's conversion to this seems superficial; the Conservative record is one of extreme centralisation; and although groups such as Charter 88 are articulate, decentralised government comes low down on their list of priorities. Tom Nairn has argued that the English metropolitan, parliamentary, monarchic 'fix' goes very deep, and I find it difficult to disagree. A recent poll showed 60% against any major regionalisation of government. Thatcher also seems to have brought to the surface a propensity to intolerance and violence which has cut across the country's previous reputation for unexcitability and the absorption of outsiders. The 'privatisation' of life doesn't leave much resilience in society when things go wrong. Enough adaptive qualities, however, remain to make some progress possible, as does the habit of the Scots and Welsh of extending nationality to incomers who are sympathetic. These are valuable advantages in what could be a difficult transition.

English provincial government hasn't been tried but that is no reason to write it off. This reluctance has to do with a lack of political imagination, as well as Thatcher's vindictiveness. The German experience proves that artificially-constructed units of government can create their own politics, provided their powers are adequate and much of the central executive is dismantled and re-erected on a regional basis. *Transpennine*, envisaging a linear city between Liverpool and Hull, is potentially a lot more 'real' than many German *Länder*. I sense that such a project, even on an *ad hoc* basis, would take off more rapidly than some neatly-structured regional division of England, bound by 'local identity', heraldry and cricket. But such an evolution shouldn't act as a brake on Scots and Welsh autonomy. In fact the achievement of this should inflict enough damage on London's power-base to provoke a general decentralisation.

We are in a tight place and have, like Peter Pienaar in John Buchan's *Greenmantle* to 'make a plan' and to create the moral values to make it work. Market forces may have their place, but salvation cannot come through resignation to them; only through knowledge, deliberate planning, austerity – a rejection of materialism – and compassion. In the 1850s the great Italian democrat Guiseppi Mazzini told the young Mark Rutherford,

> Whenever real good is done, it is by a crusade; that is to say, the cross must be raised and appeal be made to something above the people. No system based on rights will stand. Never will society be permanent until it is founded on duty.

The novel from which this quotation is taken, *Clara Hopgood*, comes from the great tradition of English radical nonconformity. Its heroine goes to Italy to fight for 'the poor people of Italy who were slaves', and dies there. The compulsion on her was a moral one, not a material one. The 'bottom line' was a conscience which Mazzini and Rutherford saw as God-given.

It's because there are things more important than the material well-being of the Scottish people that the maximum of self-government is essential. We have, in Mazzini's terms, a duty rather than a right to take part in world politics as a nation, not just to hang around the corridors of Brussels as just another region, cap in hand. The down-side of the German *Länder* is that restricted political competences *can* produce a restricted civic morality.

While two-thirds of the world's population remain, in Wall Street's euphemism, 'non-bankable', we have traditions and experiences that can help world bodies to cope with the perils that face it; we have contacts with Europe, the Third World, ideologies of ecological balance and community development which can be freed from the materialism and delusive nationalism of the London government. In Adam Ferguson's definition of the word, we suffer from the corruption of the British state. If we want to serve, we have to win free.

A centralised Britain will be the sick man of a united Europe. Whether this Europe is dominated by a centralised Germany is another issue. The *debacle* of unity has checked this bogey for the moment. Further setbacks in the east could raise nationalist emotions, but it's more likely that 'bourgeois regionalism' without a sense of European responsibility might prompt secession attempts in the most prosperous *Länder*. On the other hand, Germany is more likely to react by increasing its efforts at European unity, and in this a pluralistic, confederal Britain could be a prototype for regional co-operation. Under any circumstances, many of the deficits in infrastructure and economic policy which the present ministry has ignored will have to be remedied by European institutions.

Scotland will have to operate within this context, and if we are to be successful, our cultural and educational advantages have to be directly marketed, and not at several removes. Independence in Europe demands that we undertake the duties of a political community on the world stage. But I don't believe we can gain this necessary autonomy without sacrifice: the rejection by the political elite of that succulent image of jets, yachts and aphrodisiac power held out by the Murdochs and the Maxwells. The alternative, the creation of a more equal, more principled society, isn't glamorous or immediately rewarding, and the sacrifices necessary – measured in material terms – must continue long after autonomy has been gained. My fear remains what it was in the 1970s, that our national cause is the amateur politics of 'people who know when they're well off', to be deferred when some easier option comes up.

We owe much to the trade unions, who have planned and encouraged cooperation where business has contented itself with applauding its political masters, to local authorities, who have fought a mass of capriciously vindictive legislation to maintain a civic spirit, to the Churches, who have contributed a moral imperative lacking in the 1970s. If we believe that our ideal is up to it, we must be prepared to offer ourselves for it.

## Detmold, and a Late Score

### I

The diesel trundled slowly along the branch line, through cornfields ready for harvest and scattered with the red of poppies, behind and below was the blue haze of the Ruhrgebiet, far out of sight Bochum and that vast university of concrete towers where I'd been at a conference. We reached a quiet junction, then a line that ran by fishponds and shade trees. In the distance a forest and on the western horizon, Herman the German waving a sword against the world.

It took me ten years of my time in Germany to reach the town of Detmold, in the north of the country, near Hanover. For far longer than that period it had remained a goal, like the river that the Guru sought in *Kim*. The reason was the two serenades that Brahms composed during the 1850s when he was Court Musician to the Prince of Lippe-Detmold. They aren't among his best-known compositions, but they show the energy of his imagination, and that mixture of traditional folk-music with classical discipline which is somehow always compelling – think of Ravel's *Le Tombeau de Couperin*, Grieg's *Holberg Suite*, or Nielsen's *Springtime in Funen* – foot-tapping peasant dances which can suddenly move to a sort of solemn joy.

Anyhow, the serenades had always seemed to me to sum up the spirit of the little states of the 'good Germany', the sort of places captured by R L Stevenson in *Prince Otto*, or in the words that E M Forster gives to the father of the Schlegel sisters in *Howards End*, in his assault on the giantism of the Kaiser's *Reich*:

You only care about the things that you can use, and therefore arrange them in the following order: Money, supremely useful; intellect, rather useful; imagination, of no use at all . . . Your Pan-Germanism is no more imaginative than is our imperialism over here. It is the vice of a vulgar mind to be thrilled with bigness, to think that a thousand square miles are a thousand times more wonderful than one square mile, and that a million square miles are almost the same as heaven. That is not imagination. No, it kills it. When their poets over here try to celebrate bigness they are dead at once and naturally. Your poets too are dying, your philosophers, your musicians to whom Europe has listened for two hundred years. Gone. Gone with the little courts that nurtured them – gone with Esterhaz and Weimar. What? What's that? Your Universities? Oh yes, you have learned men, who collect more facts than do the learned men of England. They collect facts and facts, and empires of facts. But which of them will rekindle the light within?

And there it was, exactly as I had expected. The prince's waiting room, in gothic, at the station, the lime avenue, the *Jugendstil* court theatre facing the royal park, the seventeenth-century 'old palace' with its moat. Cobbled streets, three medieval churches, half-timbered houses, and a few hundred yards out of town the 'new palace', small and Italianate in the 'English' park, where Brahms had worked. The place was a gem, but it also functioned, with shops and cinemas in the centre, the market in the main square bursting with the colour and scent of fruit, cheese, new bread and flowers, almost as fine as ours in Tübingen. I thought of some Scots towns of similar size – Dumfries, say, or Kilmarnock – smashed by seventh-rate developer's architecture; grey slabs, housing inside them glitzy shopping malls which could have come from anywhere, swallowing the retail trade, the surviving streets boarded up or given over to charity shops. 'The jail might have been the infirmary, the infirmary might have been the jail, the town hall might have been either, or both, or anything else for anything that appeared to the contrary in the graces of their construction'. Thus Dickens on Coketown in 1854. Not a lot had improved in a century and a half. 'The land without imagination, the land without music?' Our most atmospheric music – the Hebrides Overture, the Scottish symphony – was composed by Brahms' older contemporary, Mendelssohn. Even *Brigadoon* came out of German-Jewish New York. But then, quite unexpectedly, I spotted a plaque on an old house by the river: 'Ferdinand Freiligrath was born here'. Freiligrath was a poet and radical, who spent much of his life in exile in Britain after the failure of

the revolutions of 1848. In that year he wrote one of the greatest
lyrics of the German working-class movement, one of whose lines
was everywhere in 1989, in the streets of Leipzig and Berlin, Prague
and Budapest: 'Trotz Alledem':

> Nur, was zerfällt, vertretet ihr!
> Seid Kasten nur, trotz alledem!
> Wir sind das Volk, die Menscheit wir,
> Sind ewig drum, trotz alledem!
> Trotz alledem und alledem:
> So kommt denn an, trotz alledem!
> Ihr hemmt uns, doch ihr zwingt uns nicht –
> Unser die Welt trotz alledem!

I don't think I have to translate. Somehow, I felt with pride and
some relief, the Scots had managed an equaliser in extra time.

## II

**Punter:** Is that you finished? Well, I'll grant you've been quite
entertaining, but what's the point? No way was that last bit a
'programme' for Scotland's future.

**CTH:** I wasn't meaning to put up a programme, but to suggest
that before we thought about organising Scotland's economy
we worked out in our own imagination where we were supposed to fit into Europe, and what sort of country we wanted
Scotland to be.

**Punter:** But are ordinary people interested in this? They want
security, a decent job, a house, and they want a car – whether
you approve of it or not.

**CTH:** Most people don't want to get involved in politics. They leave
it to the enthusiasts. But what if there's no alternative? What did
we feel like at the time of Chernobyl? Literally powerless. As
for cars: we're supposed to be building a new Kingston Bridge
in Glasgow and a second Forth Road Bridge 'to cope with
increased traffic'. These add nothing to our industrial capital.
They are a complete waste of resources which really could be
effective elsewhere – in education or research.

**Punter:** The trouble with you is that you *like* travelling around in
trains – someone else does the paying – to nice wee towns, and
you live in one yourself. Most of us live in cities because that's
where we're stuck, and if we can get our hands on a car we
get one. Have you looked at train fares in Scotland? You're
fundamentally an authoritarian. You think that MacDiarmid is
profound. Who in Wester Hailes knows anything about him?

Besides, he *hated* ordinary people. A man who said he would sacrifice God knows how many million folk for a Beethoven string quartet is a monster. And by becoming a Communist he more or less backed what he preached. All of that is now finished.

**CTH:** MacDiarmid was a poet and prophet, no more a logical thinker than Carlyle. But both of them showed the sort of potential we can be capable of. They wanted people to push their own talents to the limits, and not be mere consuming animals. And we can only do this in society. My fear is that what we could see in our 'new Europe' isn't society but private wealth *and* private poverty, both of them creeping away into their own habitations to die. This while we have the resources to *think* collectively, and therefore create something far better. So if you want cheap public transport you've got to fight for it – force Strathclyde to spend its road budget on subsidising buses and trains – not give up.

**Punter:** Where did collective thought get you? Chernobyl.

**CTH:** War and dictatorship brought us Chernobyl, and you haven't shown us how we get away from this menace. We don't, unless we act together, and those of us who are adequately well-off forego a lot of private satisfactions which are expensive and pretty pointless in favour of investment in things which meet world problems. Otherwise we're finished. Do you know the end of *The Cherry Orchard*? The estate is sold off to Lophakin, and the trees are going to be felled. All the superior folk leave, and they forget that they've locked their old servant Firs into the house. He's so doddery that he'll probably never get out, and he says 'It's as if I've never lived.' Lenin once said that it was Chekhov who made him a revolutionary – with a line like that.

**Punter:** Look what happened to him. Leningrad is St Petersburg again. The last seventy years are something the Russians could have done without.

**CTH:** But Firs' problem was there before the revolution, and it's going to loom up again. If you simply drug your 'liberated' people with Western consumer goods – McDonalds, Disney World, Coca-Cola – they'll feel as they grow old that they haven't lived, either. Anyway, as there isn't going to be enough Western affluence to go around, it could be real drugs.

**Punter:** There you go, vanishing off into some monster dystopia. All right, these problems exist, but our business is to get along from day to day, which is difficult enough in all conscience. Give people a break. I vote Labour like everyone else – that is, except you – but socialism's finished. No-one wants Utopias any more.

CTH: I'm a nationalist and a socialist. The moment I say that I feel embarrassed, knowing where that combination ended up in Germany. But German nationalism was an aggressive, militarist nationalism that excluded. And its socialism depended on plundering other people. Scottish nationalism is about how people understand and run a smallish community, without exploiting anyone. And socialism means such communities cooperating, and realising that they have common opponents in an unequal world order and wealth which has no obligations to any community. *Laisser-faire* will lead to nationalism of a sort, as the rich will make sure that the disadvantaged pick on another community as scapegoats, not on them. But when things get stuck in this groove, and lead to violence becoming epidemic, they suddenly rediscover socialism. The *Economist* regrets that there hasn't been class politics in Northern Ireland, and wants a Labour government in Israel. Socialism's like God, if it didn't exist, we'd have to invent it . . .

\* \* \* \* \* \*

KEEGAN: Sir: when you speak to me of English and Irish you forget that I am a Catholic. My country is not Ireland nor England, but the whole mighty realm of my Church. For me there are but two countries: heaven and hell; but two conditions of men: salvation and damnation. Standing here between you the Englishman, so clever in your foolishness, and this Irishman, so foolish in his cleverness, I cannot in my ignorance be sure which of you is the more deeply damned; but I should be unfaithful to my calling if I opened the gates of my heart less widely to one than to the other.

George Bernard Shaw, *John Bull's Other Island*

# Further Reading

Adam Smith Institute, *The Omega File: Scottish Policy* (1983).
John Ardagh, *Germany and the Germans* (Hamish Hamilton, 1986).
John Ardagh, *A Tale of Five Cities* (Hamish Hamilton, 1979).
Neal Ascherson, *Games with Shadows* (Radius, 1988).
Timothy Garton Ash, *We the People: the Revolution of 89* (Granta Books/Penguin, 1990).
Christoph Bertram (ed), *New Weapons and the Balance of Power* (Macmillan 1978).
Peter M Bode, *et al.*, *Alptraum Auto* (Raben, 1987).
Fernand Braudel, *The Structures of Everyday Life* (Harper Row, 1982).
Gordon Brown, *Where There is Greed* (Mainstream, 1990).
Gro Harlem Brundtland, chair, *Our Common Future: the World Commission on Environment and Development* (Oxford University Press 1987).
Ken Cargill (ed), *Scotland 2000* (BBC, 1987).
Ralf Dahrendorf, *On Britain* (BBC, 1983).
Ralf Dahrendorf, *Reflections on the Revolution in Europe* (Chatto, 1990).
George Elder Davie, *The Scottish Enlightenment* (Polygon, 1991).
Economist Intelligence Unit, *World Outlook* (1989, 1990, 1991).
Hans Magnus Enzensberger, *Europe! Europe!* (Radius, 1989).
Fabian Society, *The Debt Crisis: the Third World and British Banks* (1987).
Kevin Featherstone, *The Successful Manager's Guide to 1992* (Fontana, 1990).
Francis Fukuyama, *The End of History* (1990).
Peter Glotz, *Der Deutschen Recht* (DVA Stuttgart, 1992).
Michael Harrington, *The Next Left* (I B Tauris, 1987).
Christopher Harvie, *The Centre of Things: Political Fiction in Britain from Disraeli to the Present* (Unwin Hyman, 1991).
Christopher Harvie, *Imagining an European Future* (Scottish Council: Development and Industry, 1988).

Christopher Harvie, *Europe and the Scottish Nation* (Scottish Centre for Economic and Social Research, 1989; new edition, 1991).

Roy Jenkins, *European Diary* (Weidenfeld and Nicholson, 1989).

Michael Keating, *State and Regional Nationalism* (Harvester, 1989).

Paul Kennedy, *The Rise and Fall of the Great Powers* (1988; Fontana Press, 1989).

Landeszentrale für politische Bildung Baden-Württemberg, *The German Southwest* (Kohlhammer, 1991).

Landeszentrale für politische Bildung Baden-Württemberg, *Baden-Württemberg: eine kleine politische Landeskunde* (1991).

Walter Laqueur, *A Continent Astray, Europe, 1970-1978* (Oxford University Press, 1979).

Hans-Werner Ludwig and Lothar Fietz (eds), *Regionalism and the Lyric in Europe* (Attempto, 1991).

David Marsh, *The New Germany at the Crossroads* (Radius, 1990).

Kenneth O Morgan, *The People's Peace: Britain, 1945-90* (Oxford University Press, 1990).

Tom Nairn, *The Enchanted Glass: Britain and its Monarchy* (Radius 1988).

National Bureau of Economic Research (NBER), *The United States and the World Economy* (1987).

John Osmond, *Alternatives: New Approaches to Health, Education, Energy, the Family and the Aquarian Age* (Thorsons, 1984).

Jonathon Porritt, *Green Politics* (Fontana, 1990).

Jim Sillars, *Scotland: the Case for Optimism* (Polygon, 1986).

Scottish Trades Union Congress, *Scotland: a Land fit for People* (1987).

Keith Sword (ed), *The Times Guide to Eastern Europe: the Changing Face of the Warsaw Pact* (Times Books, 1990).

Martin Wiener, *English Culture and the Decline of the Industrial Spirit* (Cambridge, 1981).

Patrick Wright, *On Living in an Old Country* (Verso, 1985).

# Index